the international cookbook
for kids

by Matthew Locricchio

Photographs by
Jack McConnell

two lions

acknowledgments

Cookbooks are the result of great teamwork

and the cooperation of many people, and *The International Cookbook for Kids* owes a world of thanks to the members of the Recipe Testers Club and their adult assistant chefs, whose testing, comments, and suggestions were invaluable in creating this book. They are: Saun Ellis, Francisco Drohojowski, Sonia Drohojowska, and Danny and Nico of Sherman, Connecticut; Diane Carter, Molly Hall, and Sadie Hall of Santa Cruz, California; Virginia and Paul, Nikolas, and assistant Joey Zerang of Glenview, Illinois; Linda Sproule of New York City; Mary Rich and Matthew Zimmerman of Riverdale, New York; Lydia Aultman and William Aultman of Hudson, New York; Douglas and Sophie Madach and Victoria Aucion of River Ridge, Louisiana; and Lisa Cooper-Weinburg and Joshua Weinburg of Prattsburg, New York. My profound thanks go to my dear friend, the late Marta Hallett, of Traverse City, Michigan, whose team testing of the Chinese dishes helped shape the final recipes. A special thank you to Carlos Guiterez of the Mexican Cultural Institute for helping with my research, and John Strand for his recipe archives. Many thanks also to Lydia Aultman for her nutritional guidance; Dr. David Castronuovo for his help with my Italian; Xiuwen Wu, PhD, College of Education, Michigan State University; and Delores Custer and Peter DeLuca of Vincent's Meat Market on Arthur Avenue, Bronx, New York. I must also extend my gratitude to the works of Julia Child, Paul Bocouse, Waverly Root, Burton Anderson, Marcella Hazen, Pellegrino Artusi, Rick Bayless, Elizabeth David, Dianna Kennedy, Jean Andrews, Nina Simonds, and Eileen Yin-Fei-Lo, whose works have inspired my cooking over the years and of course *The International Cookbook for Kids* itself. Thanks also to Mr. Jack McConnell for his outstanding photographs and rock-solid temperament; his assistant John Addario; and to Marie Hirschfeld for her great food styling and endurance during our marathon sessions. I am indebted to my family and friends who have been so supportive during the creation of this book. Special thanks to Sharon Bowers; Anahid Hamparian, for her excellent art direction; Sonia Chaghatzbanian for her outstanding design; and to the great people at Marshall Cavendish for having the good sense to publish the book; to my editor Margery Cuyler, who believed it was time for an international cookbook for kids and worked incredibly hard to make it happen. Most of all my thanks to Richard.

two lions

Text copyright © 2004 by Matthew Locricchio
Food photographs © 2004 by Jack McConnell, McConnell, McNamara & Company
First Amazon Children's Publishing paperback edition, 2012
Art director for food photography: Matthew Locricchio

Published by Two Lions, New York
www.apub.com
Amazon, the Amazon logo, and Two Lions are trademarks of
Amazon.com, Inc., or its affiliates.

Library of Congress Cataloging-in-Publication Data

Locricchio, Matthew.
The international cookbook for kids / by Matthew Locricchio, Marshall Cavendish.
p. cm.
Includes index.
978-0-7614-5185-3 (hardcover) 978-0-7614-6313-9 (paperback)
1. Cookery, International—Juvenile literature. I. Cavendish, Marshall. II. Title.

TX725.A1L62 2004
641.5'622—dc22
2004005894
Book design by Sonia Chaghatzbanian
Editor: Margery Cuyler

Printed in China

For my mother, Virginia Mary Locricchio,
who taught me that anything is possible

contents

Italy

China

Mexico

vegetables and side dishes

main dishes

France

desserts

Introduction

The International Cookbook for Kids is for young chefs who want to increase their cooking skills by using classic recipes from Italy, France, China, and Mexico—"the big four" of world cooking. This book offers a hands-on tour of these cuisines. You'll recognize some of each country's most famous dishes. The recipes range from simple to challenging. The directions are easy to follow; the ingredients are available in most supermarkets; and the results will make your guests happy. The recipes were tested by the members of my own Recipe Testers Club, comprised of cooks just like you, who prepared dishes in kitchens probably a lot like yours.

Many people today are so busy that they depend on fast, processed, frozen, and canned foods for their meals. As a result, they simply don't know how to cook and have never experienced the pure pleasure of serving a successful meal to friends and family.

My early childhood memories revolve around the kitchen. My Sicilian-American parents were professional cooks who came from a culture that celebrated food. I can recall my mother's mother sitting me on a stool by her black iron stove while she stirred a big pot of pasta sauce or soup. Every now and then, she'd give me a taste of what she was making. But it was really my parents who instilled a love for cooking that has lasted my whole life. Together we prepared many dishes in our kitchen. That's why I recommend that you have at least one adult assistant chef when you prepare the recipes in this book. Family or friends cooking together make the whole experience just that much more enjoyable.

I have chosen classic international recipes because they have survived the test of time. When a professional chef studies the art of cooking, he or she learns that French, Italian, Chinese, and, more recently, Mexican recipes are taught in the best culinary schools around the world. So much of American cooking is influenced by the big four that if you want to learn how to cook, you should first learn the basics from these four cuisines. Once you master the recipes and culinary techniques in this book, you will be able to accomplish almost anything in the kitchen.

I always recommend that you use fresh ingredients. If you're not sure when something is fresh, just ask. Don't be afraid to inquire when the fish was delivered or when the vegetables arrived in the market. Although not all the dishes are low-fat or low-calorie or low-carb, they are healthful. Even if you are a vegetarian, you will find recipes without meat or with suggestions to prepare a meatless version of the dish.

People all over the world have shared the pleasures of eating since the beginning of time. When you cook for someone, you are offering them a creative, caring gift. Although cooking can involve hard work, it is also fun, never boring, and always rewarding. Why go out to find entertainment? The best breakfasts, luncheons, and dinners can happen right in your own kitchen. Good food, family, and friends are the ingredients for a great time to be shared by all.

Happy cooking!
—*Matthew Locricchio*

Before You Begin

A Word about Safety

- Ask an adult to be your assistant chef. To ensure your safety, steps in a recipe are best done with the help of an adult, like handling pots of boiling water or hot cooking oils. Good cooking is about teamwork. With an adult assistant to help, you've got the makings of a perfect team.

- Wash your hands first and often when you are working with food. Washing under hot water with lots of soap for twenty seconds will greatly reduce the risk of transferring bacteria from your hands to the food. Wash your hands again after you handle raw meats, poultry, fish, or tofu.

- Always start with a clean kitchen before you begin any recipe, and leave the kitchen clean when you're done.

- Read the entire recipe before you start to prepare it and have a clear understanding of how the recipe works. If something is not clear, ask your teammate to explain it.

- Dress the part of a chef. Wear an apron. Tie back long hair so that it's out of your food and away from open flames. Why not do what a chef does and wear a clean hat to cover your hair?

- Pot holders and hot pads are your friends. The hands they save may be your own. Use them only if they are dry. Using wet holders on a hot pot can cause a serious burn!

- Keep the handles of the pots and pans turned toward the middle of the stove. That way you won't accidentally hit them and knock over pots of hot food. Always use pot holders to lift a hot lid or move a pan on the stove or in the oven.

- Remember to turn off the stove and oven when you are finished cooking. This sounds like a simple idea, but it's easy to forget.

Be Sharp about Knives

- A simple rule about knife safety is that your hands work as a team. One hand grips the handle and operates the knife while the other guides the food you are cutting. The hand holding the food should never come close to the blade of the knife. Keep the fingertips that hold the food slightly curved and out of the path of the blade, and use your thumb to keep the food steady. Go slowly. There is no reason to chop very fast.

- Always hold the knife handle with dry hands. If your hands are wet, the knife might slip. Work on a cutting board, never a tabletop or countertop.

- Never place sharp knives in a sink full of soapy water, where they could be hidden from view. Someone reaching into the water might get hurt.

- Take good care of your knives. Good chef knives should be washed by hand, never in a dishwasher.

soups

Chicken Stock *Fond Blanc de Volaille*

There is nothing that can compare with the flavor of homemade chicken stock. It is easy to make, so you can always have it on hand when you need it. You can buy canned or frozen stock and still get good flavor, but using homemade is the best way to control the amount of salt in any recipe using chicken stock. This recipe will introduce you to a *bouquet garni*, a tiny bundle of herbs and spices that the French use to flavor their dishes.

Serves 6

ingredients

Stock
1 whole chicken or chicken parts,
   wings or legs (3 to 3 1/2 pounds)
1 medium-size onion
2 carrots unpeeled
2 stalks celery
3 quarts cold water
1 1/2 teaspoons salt

Bouquet garni
5- to 6-inch square cheesecloth
3 sprigs fresh flat-leaf parsley
1 bay leaf
3 or 4 black peppercorns
2 or 3 thyme sprigs
cotton string

On your mark, get set . . .

- Rinse the chicken and place it in a large stockpot.

- Chop the onion (no need to peel it), carrots, and celery, and add them to the pot.

- To make the *bouquet garni*: Lay the cheesecloth square on a clean work surface. Place all the ingredients for the bouquet inside the square, tie it into a bundle with the string at the top, and place it in the pot. If you make the string long enough, you can tie the bundle to the handle of the pot, which makes it really easy to remove at the end of the cooking.

Cook!

- Add the cold water and salt to the pot, and bring to a boil on medium-high heat. As the liquid comes to a boil, use a large spoon to skim off any foam or impurities that rise to the surface. Reduce the heat to low, partially cover, and simmer the stock for 1 1/2 hours.

- Get an adult to help you remove the pot from the heat and drain the stock into a colander lined with cheesecloth and placed over a large bowl or pot. Gently press on the ingredients to extract all the flavor.

- When the cooked ingredients are cool enough to handle, discard the vegetables and the *bouquet garni*. The chicken in this recipe can be removed from the bone after it is cooked and used cold in salads or for delicious sandwiches.

- Cool the stock for 20 minutes, then cover and fully chill it in the refrigerator for at least a few hours, and remove any fat that has risen to the top of the stock. If you are using the stock immediately, skim the fat off the top with a large spoon and discard.

What Does "Organic" Mean?

Organic fruits and vegetables are grown without the use of chemical pesticides or chemical fertilizers and as a result produce a product that has less of a negative impact on the environment. Organic poultry and meats are raised without the use of antibiotics or growth hormones. Many people believe that organic products are healthier for you and taste better than non-organic products. If organic chickens and produce are available in your area, why not try them and see if they really do taste better? As a rule, organic products are expensive, so keep your budget in mind when you are shopping.

chef's tip

THE FINISHED CHICKEN STOCK WILL KEEP FOR UP TO ONE WEEK IN THE REFRIGERATOR IN AN AIRTIGHT CONTAINER, OR IT CAN BE POURED INTO SMALLER PLASTIC CONTAINERS WITH TIGHT-FITTING LIDS AND FROZEN FOR UP TO THREE MONTHS. TO THAW, PLACE THE CONTAINER UPSIDE DOWN UNDER COLD RUNNING WATER AND PRESS THE BOTTOM TO PUSH OUT THE FROZEN STOCK. HEAT THE STOCK IN A COVERED PAN ON LOW HEAT UNTIL IT MELTS. CHICKEN STOCK CAN ALSO BE THAWED OVERNIGHT IN THE REFRIGERATOR. *NEVER THAW CHICKEN STOCK ON THE COUNTER OR AT ROOM TEMPERATURE.*

Rich Meat Broth *Il Brodo*

When you look at this recipe and see that it takes three hours to cook, don't turn the page. This rich broth, or stock, is used for making soups and sauces. You will find that many recipes use broth for flavoring instead of plain water. The broth will keep in the refrigerator for three days, or you can freeze it for up to six months. For some more ways to use broth, look at the chef's tip at the end of the recipe.

Makes 1/2 gallon

ingredients

2 to 3 pounds beef bones with meat
2 to 3 pounds chicken wings, necks, or thighs (or a combination of all three)
2 stalks celery, broken into large chunks
2 carrots unpeeled, broken into large chunks
1 onion with skin, cut into quarters
1 large tomato, cut into quarters, or 1/2 cup canned tomatoes
2 whole cloves garlic with skin
1/2 cup fresh Italian parsley
10 cups cold water (2 1/2 quarts)

On your mark, get set, cook!

- Place all the ingredients except the water in a large pot.

- Add the water and bring to a boil. This will take 20 to 30 minutes. As the liquid comes to a boil, use a large spoon to skim off any foam or impurities that rise to the top.

- Cover the pot, leaving the lid slightly ajar. Reduce the heat to simmer and let cook for 2 to 3 hours.

- Turn off the heat. Ask your adult assistant to strain the broth through a colander into a heatproof bowl or pan.

- When the cooked ingredients have cooled enough to handle, discard.

- Let the broth cool and then refrigerate or freeze. Any fat in the broth will collect at the top and should be removed and discarded.

chef's tip

For a simple and flavorful soup, try this: Place 6 cups Rich Meat Broth in a saucepan, add 1/4 cup rice, and bring to a boil. Reduce the heat and simmer for 20 minutes, or until the rice is tender. Serve hot with freshly grated Parmesan cheese. Serves 4. Or: Place 4 cups Rich Meat Broth in a saucepan. Add 1 1/2 cups frozen tortellini (a pasta filled with meat or cheese, available in Italian food stores or well-stocked supermarkets). Bring to a boil, then reduce the heat and simmer for 12 to 15 minutes, or until the tortellini are just tender. Serve hot with freshly grated Parmesan cheese. Serves 2 to 4.

Homemade Vegetable Stock
Jia Chang Su Cai Tang

Just like chicken stock, vegetable stock can be bought in cans, but give this recipe a try and see how good the real thing can taste! This recipe makes 1/2 gallon of stock.

---

ingredients

6 carrots
3 stalks celery
1 yellow onion, cut into quarters
3 green onions
6 leaves iceberg lettuce (or your choice of lettuce)

3 slices fresh ginger, about 1/2 inch thick and the size of a quarter
1/2 pound fresh mushrooms (optional)
1 tablespoon salt (optional)
10 cups cold water (2 1/2 quarts)

On your mark, get set . . .

• Wash all the vegetables. Wipe off any dirt from the mushrooms with a dry paper towel. You don't have to peel the carrots or the onions—the skins will give the stock extra flavor.

• Chop the vegetables into large chunks.

Cook!

• Place all the ingredients in a large pot.

• Bring to a boil over high heat, then reduce the heat to low and simmer for 1 1/2 hours. With a large spoon, remove any foam that rises to the surface of the liquid as it cooks. Discard the foam.

• When the stock has finished cooking, turn off the heat. Ask your adult assistant to help you pour it through a colander lined with cheesecloth.

• Discard the vegetables.

• Let the stock cool, uncovered, for 20 minutes, then cover and refrigerate.

chef's tip

VEGETABLE STOCK CAN BE REFRIGERATED IN AN AIRTIGHT CONTAINER FOR UP TO SEVEN DAYS. IT CAN ALSO BE FROZEN IN SMALLER PLASTIC CONTAINERS WITH TIGHT-FITTING LIDS FOR UP TO THREE MONTHS. TO THAW, PLACE THE CONTAINER UPSIDE DOWN UNDER COLD RUNNING WATER AND PRESS THE BOTTOM TO PUSH OUT THE FROZEN STOCK. PLACE THE STOCK IN A PAN ON THE STOVE. HEAT, COVERED, ON LOW HEAT UNTIL THE STOCK MELTS. IT CAN ALSO BE THAWED OVERNIGHT IN THE REFRIGERATOR. NEVER THAW VEGETABLE STOCK ON THE COUNTER OR AT ROOM TEMPERATURE.

Vegetable Soup *Il Minestrone*

Minestrone means "big hearty soup." You will find different versions of this soup in every region of Italy. This classic recipe comes from Piedmont, in the north of Italy, and is considered by many Italians to be their country's most famous soup. For the broth, try making your own meat broth using the recipe on page 14. You can also use canned low-sodium beef or chicken broth. To make this recipe vegetarian, use vegetable broth and omit the bacon.

Serves 8

ingredients

2 tablespoons butter
2 tablespoons extra virgin olive oil
2 slices thick-cut bacon (optional)
1 medium-size onion
2 medium-size potatoes
4 small carrots
3 stalks celery
2 medium-size zucchini
¼ medium-size head savoy or regular cabbage
2 cloves garlic
1½ cups canned cannellini beans, drained

1 cup canned chopped Italian tomatoes with the tomato juice
½ tablespoon salt
½ teaspoon freshly ground pepper
6 cups homemade Chicken or Vegetable Broth, pages 12 and 16, or canned low-sodium
½ cup small dried pasta (small seashell, mini-elbow, or ditalini pasta)
freshly grated Parmigiano-Reggiano cheese for serving

On your mark, get set . . .

- Measure the butter and olive oil and set aside.

- Slice the bacon into small pieces.

- Peel the onion and chop into small pieces.

- Wash and cut the potatoes, unpeeled, in half lengthwise. Lay the flat side down and cut each half into slices, then cut the slices into small chunks.

- Wash the carrots, celery, and zucchini, and chop into bite-size pieces.

- Remove any limp outside leaves from the cabbage. Remove the white core at the base. Cut the cabbage into quarters. Chop the cabbage into small pieces and measure 2 cups.

- Crush, peel, and chop the garlic.

Cook!

- In a pot large enough to hold all the ingredients (6- to 8-quart), heat the butter and olive oil over medium-low heat.

- When the butter is melted, add the bacon, onion, and garlic. Cook for 5 to 7 minutes, or until the onion and garlic turn a soft golden color and the bacon just starts to brown.

- Add the potatoes, carrots, celery, zucchini, cabbage, cannellini beans, tomatoes, salt, and pepper. Stir well. Cook for 10 to 12 minutes, stirring occasionally.

- Add the broth. Raise the heat to medium-high and bring to a boil. Skim off any foam that rises to the top. You will need to skim the soup a couple of times as it is cooking.

- Reduce the heat to low, cover the pot with the lid slightly ajar, and simmer gently for 30 to 40 minutes.

- Add the pasta, raise the heat to medium, and cook for another 8 to 10 minutes, or until the pasta is tender.

- Serve hot with grated Parmigiano-Reggiano cheese.

(See pages 10-11 for photo.)

chef's tip

WASH THE VEGETABLES VERY WELL, ESPECIALLY THE ZUCCHINI. THERE IS NO NEED TO PEEL THEM (EXCEPT THE ONION). THE SKINS ADD LOTS OF FLAVOR, COLOR, AND NUTRIENTS TO THE SOUP.

Tortilla Soup *Sopa de Tortilla*

What's the perfect thing to do with leftover tortillas? Make tortilla soup, of course. This classic soup of Mexico is so popular that each culinary region has its own version.

Serves 6

ingredients

4 to 6 leftover corn tortillas (See page 162)
1 medium-size white onion
2 cloves garlic
8 ounces Monterey Jack or Mexican queso fresco cheese
1 lime

1 small ripe tomato or 1/2 cup canned tomatoes, undrained
1/3 cup corn or canola oil
6 cups Chicken Stock, homemade, page 12, or canned low-sodium
1 dried pasilla or ancho chile

On your mark, get set . . .

- Stack the tortillas and cut them into strips about 1/4 inch wide. Let them air-dry on the counter while you prepare the rest of the ingredients.

- Peel and slice the onion into thin slices.

- Peel the garlic and leave whole.

- Cut the cheese into small cubes and set aside.

- Cut the lime into 6 wedges and set aside.

- If using a fresh tomato, wash it and cut out the stem circle at the top. Cut the tomato into quarters. If using canned tomatoes, measure 1/2 cup, undrained.

Cook!

- Heat 1 tablespoon of the oil in a 4-quart heavy-bottomed pot on medium-low heat.

- Add the sliced onion and whole garlic cloves. Cook for 8 to 10 minutes, or until golden brown.

- Ask your adult assistant to help with the next steps.

- Add the cooked onion and garlic along with the tomato to the jar of a blender.

- Press the lid almost completely in place, leaving it slightly ajar. Blend at low speed for a few seconds. Now press the lid firmly in place and blend at high speed for about 10 to 15 seconds, or until liquefied.

- Heat another 1 tablespoon of the oil in the pot for 30 seconds, then pour in the tomato mixture from the blender. Have a lid close by, as the mixture will bubble and boil when it hits the hot oil. Cover the pot for a few seconds to prevent spattering.

- Remove the cover, and stir and cook the tomato mixture on low heat for about 5 minutes as it thickens.

- Add the chicken stock and bring to a boil. Reduce the heat to low and simmer for 20 to 30 minutes.

- In the meantime, heat the remaining oil in a 10-inch frying pan on medium heat.

- Add the tortilla strips, a few at a time, and fry until crispy. Remove with a metal slotted spoon and drain on paper towels. Repeat this step until all the tortilla strips are fried.

- Cut the top off the dried chile and run a knife along the side to open the chile like a book. Remove the seeds and veins.

- Cut the chile into 1-inch-wide strips.

- Reheat the oil on medium heat for 30 to 40 seconds.

- Fry the chile pieces for about 30 seconds to crisp them. Remove the chile and drain on paper towels.

- You are now ready to serve the soup. Add the tortilla strips to the simmering soup. Place a few cheese cubes in each individual bowl. Pour the hot soup on top and serve. Pass the chile strips and lime wedges at the table, and let your guests add them if they wish.

Onion Soup

Soupe à l'Oignon Gratinée

The story goes that one of France's most famous chefs created this soup in the fourteenth century, hoping to please the king. And that is just what he did! As you prepare this most famous of all soups, the wonderful aroma of onions gently cooking in butter will fill your kitchen. Try making it with homemade Chicken Stock (page 12). Served with French bread, it becomes a complete meal. To make this recipe vegetarian, substitute vegetable stock for the chicken or beef stock.

Serves 6

ingredients

4 medium-size onions (about 2 pounds)
4 tablespoons butter
1 teaspoon salt
4 cups homemade Chicken Stock, page 12, or canned low-sodium chicken, beef, or vegetable broth

1 tablespoon flour
freshly ground black pepper to taste
6 slices French or Italian bread, ½ inch thick
1½ cups Gruyère or Parmesan cheese (about 6 ounces)

On your mark, get set . . .

- Peel the onions and cut them into 1/2-inch slices. Measure 6 cups and set aside.

- You will need 6 individual ovenproof soup bowls that can go under the broiler or a large ovenproof casserole, which will work just as well.

Cook!

- Melt the butter in a 6-quart heavy-bottomed pan on low heat.

- Add the onion slices and salt, and cook for 20 minutes with the pan partially covered. Remove the lid and continue to cook until the onions caramelize to a soft brown color. It is not necessary to stir the onions constantly. Every so often, give them a stir and check to make sure they are not burning; if so, reduce the heat a little.

- Toward the end of the cooking time, bring the stock to a simmer on low heat.

- After the onions have changed color and are very limp, sprinkle on the flour and mix in well. Continue to cook for another minute or so.

- Add the onions to the simmering stock and raise the heat to medium. Add the pepper and bring to a boil.

- Once the soup boils, reduce the heat to simmer and cook slowly for 40 minutes.

- Preheat the oven to 400°F.

- Lay the bread slices on a baking sheet and bake for 10 to 15 minutes, or until the bread is brown and toasted. Remove from the oven and set aside.

- Grate the cheese, measure 1 1/2 cups, and set aside.

- If preparing individual servings: Light the broiler in the oven. Place the oven-proof soup bowls on a strong metal tray. Place 1 slice toasted bread in each bowl, breaking it to fit if necessary. Ladle the hot soup into the bowls, filling them three-quarters full. Completely cover the top of the soup in each bowl with grated cheese.

- Have an adult assistant help you place the bowls under the broiler, and broil for about 3 minutes. The cheese will melt and become bubbly and golden brown. Keep a close watch on it so it doesn't burn.

- Turn off the broiler, remove the tray of bowls, and serve the soup hot.

- If using a large casserole: Place the toasted bread in the bottom of the oven-proof casserole. Add the soup. Cover the top of the casserole with the grated cheese.

- Bake for 10 minutes at 400°F. Turn the oven to broil and melt and brown the cheese. This will take 3 to 4 minutes. Keep a close watch on it so it doesn't burn.

- Turn off the broiler. Remove the casserole from the oven and serve hot.

chef's tip

IF MAKING THE SOUP AHEAD OF TIME, PREPARE THE SOUP, LET IT COOL, AND REFRIGERATE IT. WHEN YOU ARE READY TO SERVE THE SOUP, GENTLY REHEAT IT ON LOW HEAT, ASSEMBLE WITH THE BREAD AND CHEESE, AND BAKE/BROIL AS DIRECTED ABOVE.

Hot and Sour Soup *Suan La Tang*

This is one of the most recognizable soups in Chinese cooking. It is said to have originated in Beijing, though the Szechwan and Hunan cooks in China insist this dish comes from their provinces. Once you try your own homemade version, you will want to claim it as your own dish, too. If you can't find dried shiitake mushrooms, you can substitute fresh ones. Just follow the note at the end of the recipe. The white pepper gives the soup its heat, so you can add more or less of it as you like.

Serves 6

ingredients

4 dried shiitake mushrooms
¼ pound boneless pork loin, slightly frozen
3 ounces firm tofu
1 green onion
½ cup bamboo shoots
4 cups homemade Chicken Stock, page 12, or canned low-sodium
1 teaspoon salt

2 teaspoons soy sauce
1/4 teaspoon ground white pepper (optional)
2 tablespoons white vinegar
1/2 cup frozen sweet peas
2 tablespoons cornstarch mixed with 3 tablespoons water
1 egg, slightly beaten
1 teaspoon sesame oil

On your mark...

• Soak the dried mushrooms in ½ cup warm water for 20 to 30 minutes.*

• Cut the pork into thin slices. Stack the slices of pork a few at a time and cut into slivers.

• Cut the tofu into long strips and then into 2-inch squares.

• Finely chop the green onion.

• Rinse the bamboo shoots in a hand strainer under cold running water to remove any bitter taste. Then cut them into thin slices.

Get set...

• Drain the mushrooms, saving the liquid. Using a pair of kitchen scissors, cut off the stems and discard. Cut the mushroom caps into thin slices.

• Line up these ingredients on your countertop: chicken stock, mushroom liquid, pork, salt, soy sauce, mushrooms, bamboo shoots, tofu, white pepper, vinegar, frozen peas, cornstarch mixture, egg, green onion, sesame oil.

Cook!

- Pour the chicken stock and mushroom liquid into a 4-quart pot.

- Add the pork, salt, soy sauce, mushrooms, and bamboo shoots. Bring to a boil over high heat. Then reduce the heat to low, cover, and simmer for 5 minutes.

- Add the tofu, white pepper, vinegar, and frozen peas. Raise the heat to high and bring the soup back to a boil.

- Stir the cornstarch and water to recombine and slowly pour into the boiling soup. Gently stir the soup for a few seconds as it thickens.

- Carefully stir in the egg and cook for 30 seconds.

- Turn off the heat and add the green onion and sesame oil. Stir and serve hot in bowls.

chef's tip

To make this soup vegetarian: Omit the pork and egg; use vegetable stock instead of chicken stock; use 6 ounces tofu, 2 green onions, and 2 teaspoons of salt.

*NOTE: If you can't find dried shiitake mushrooms, you can substitute fresh mushrooms. Look for fresh shiitake or small Portobello mushrooms. Remove and discard the stems, brush any dirt from the mushrooms with a dry paper towel, and slice the mushroom caps before adding to the pot. It is not necessary to soak fresh mushrooms, so you can omit the mushroom liquid from the recipe.

appetizers and snacks

Egg Rolls *Chun Juan*

Egg rolls, a creation from Canton, are actually part of a delicious collection of appetizers called dim sum. This recipe is made without deep-frying. Instead, the egg rolls are pan-fried. They are light, delicious, and really fun to make.

Serves 12

ingredients

½ pound fresh or frozen shrimp (if frozen, thaw before using)
½ small head cabbage
1 stalk celery
3 green onions
2 slices fresh ginger, unpeeled
1 clove garlic, unpeeled
8 cups cold water (2 quarts)

1 tablespoon sugar
4 teaspoons salt
1/2 cup canola oil
1 tablespoon soy sauce
1 teaspoon sesame oil
12 egg roll or spring roll wrappers
1 egg, slightly beaten
1 cup bean sprouts

On your mark...

- Peel the shrimp and discard the shells. Cut the shrimp in half lengthwise. Rinse under cold running water, and pull out the vein and discard. Refrigerate the cut shrimp.

- Cut the cabbage into thin slices and measure 2 cups.

- Cut the celery into 1/4-inch pieces.

- Cut the green onions into 1/4-inch pieces.

- Using the flat side of a knife, crush the slices of ginger and the garlic.

- Fill a large pot with 8 cups water and add the ginger and garlic.

- Add the sugar and 2 teaspoons of the salt. Cover and bring to a boil.

- Add the shrimp and cook, uncovered, for 1 minute, or just until the shrimp turn pink. Using a slotted spoon or Chinese strainer, remove the shrimp and place them in a colander. After the shrimp are drained, place them in a large bowl.

- Remove the ginger and garlic from the water and discard.

- Bring the same pot of water back to a boil and add the cabbage and celery. Cook for 1 to 2 minutes, or until the cabbage is bright green.

- Drain the vegetables in a colander. Using the back of a large slotted spoon, press down on the cabbage and celery to remove any extra water. Give the colander a few gentle tosses to remove the last of the water. Then add the cabbage and celery to the shrimp.

Get Set...

- Heat a wok on medium-high heat for 1 minute. Add 1 tablespoon of the canola oil. Heat for 30 seconds.

- Add the sliced green onions and stir-fry for 1 minute.

- Now add the shrimp and vegetable mixture, soy sauce, sesame oil, and the remaining 2 teaspoons of salt. Stir-fry for 1 minute, mixing all the ingredients together.

- Empty the stir-fry ingredients into a colander to drain. These ingredients are the filling for the egg rolls.

- On a clean surface, lay out 1 egg roll wrapper as if it were a baseball diamond. Home plate is the corner facing you. Cover the rest of the wrappers so they won't dry out.

- Using a pastry brush, paint a little of the beaten egg all along the outside edge of the wrapper.

- Place about 1½ tablespoons of the filling in a line between first and third base. Add a small bunch of the bean sprouts on top of the filling.

- Beginning at home plate, roll up halfway, gently packing the filling inside. Tuck the first- and third-base corners into the center and finish rolling to second base. You just made an egg roll!

- Place on a platter, cover with plastic wrap, and keep cold while you make the rest. Repeat until all the egg rolls are made.

Cook!

- Preheat the oven to 200°F.

- Heat 2 tablespoons of the canola oil in a wok or frying pan for about 30 seconds.

- Using a pair of tongs to lift and turn the egg rolls, carefully pan-fry them—1 at a time in a wok or 2 at a time in a frying pan—until they are golden brown and crispy. This will take about 2 to 3 minutes each. Add the remaining oil to the pan as needed.

- Let the finished egg rolls drain on paper towels. Then keep them warm in the oven until all of them are ready.

- Serve hot with a dipping sauce.

(See pages 28-29 for photo.)

chef's tip

To make the egg rolls vegetarian, omit the shrimp and use spring roll wrappers. Spring roll wrappers are more fragile than egg roll wrappers because they are made without eggs. Handle them carefully so they won't tear.

dipping sauces

Soy and Ginger
1 tablespoon soy sauce
1 teaspoon fresh ginger, minced, or chopped very finely
1 tablespoon sesame oil

Duck Sauce and Vinegar
2 tablespoons duck sauce
1 tablespoon rice wine vinegar

Cold Sesame Noodles *Liang Mian*

This recipe comes from the provinces of Hunan and Szechwan. The weather there gets hot and sticky in the summer months, and cold dishes are just the right thing for a refreshing summer meal. Cold Sesame Noodles can start a meal, make a wonderful lunch, or be served as part of a large banquet. Any way you serve it, this dish will be asked for again and again. If you wish to make the noodles vegetarian, use vegetable stock instead of chicken stock.

Serves 6

ingredients

½ pound angel hair pasta
1 tablespoon sesame oil

dressing

½ cup chunky peanut butter
½ cup homemade Chicken or
   Vegetable Stock, pages 12 and
   16, or canned low-sodium
3 tablespoons soy sauce

2 tablespoons sesame oil
1 tablespoon Worcestershire sauce
1 tablespoon sugar
½ teaspoon ground white pepper

topping

1 green onion
¼ cup chopped peanuts
2 tablespoons sesame seeds

On your mark, get set, cook!

- Cook the pasta according to the package directions. Drain in a colander, then toss with 1 tablespoon sesame oil. Refrigerate for at least 1 hour.

- Place the ingredients for the dressing in a quart jar with a lid, and shake until well blended. Refrigerate until ready to serve.

- Mince the green onion, measure about ¼ cup, and refrigerate.

- Measure out the chopped peanuts, and toast the sesame seeds in an oven or a toaster oven 4 to 5 minutes.

- To serve, arrange the cold pasta on a serving platter. Pour the dressing over the pasta and sprinkle the green onion, chopped peanuts, and sesame seeds on top.

Ham and Cheese Crunches
Croque-Monsieur

The cafés and bistros in Paris are busy at lunchtime with large numbers of local diners and tourists. Smart Parisians know the right places to find appealing sandwiches. First served in 1910 at a Parisian café, this version of a ham and cheese sandwich is still popular today. The name *croque-monsieur* literally means "crunch-sir." Try this popular version of a bistro recipe and you will say, *"Vive la France."*

Serves 4-6

ingredients

8 slices thin sandwich bread
4 slices smoked or boiled ham
  (1 ounce each)
4 ounces Gruyère or Swiss cheese

3 tablespoons milk
3 tablespoons melted butter

On your mark, get set . . .

- Preheat the oven to 400°F.

- Cut away the crusts of the bread with a sharp knife. Discard the crusts. Lay 4 of the slices on a small baking sheet.

- Cut the ham so it neatly fits the slices of bread, with none extending over the sides. You will probably have more than one layer of ham, but that is okay.

- Grate the Gruyère or Swiss cheese into a small bowl. Add the milk and combine with the cheese.

- Spoon one-quarter of the cheese mixture on top of the ham on one sandwich, and cover with a slice of bread.

- With a pastry brush, butter the top slice. Carefully turn the sandwich over and butter the bottom slice.

- Repeat these steps to assemble the other 3 crunches.

Cook!

- Place the baking sheet in the oven and bake the sandwiches for 10 to 15 minutes, or until the cheese melts and the bread just begins to brown.

- Turn the oven to broil. Brown the sandwiches under the broiler for 1 minute on each side. If necessary, reshape the sandwiches with a spatula after you turn them, tapping in the sides like a deck of cards. Be careful not to let them burn.

- Lift the finished crunches off the baking sheet with a spatula to a serving dish. Let cool for a moment, cut into quarters, and serve hot.

Bacon and Egg Custard Tart

Quiche Lorraine

This classic recipe from the region of Alsace-Lorraine dates back to the sixteenth century when, so they say, Quiche Lorraine was created to celebrate the coming of spring and served on May Day. It is simple to make, beautiful to look at, and delicious. That is probably why it has been a favorite for centuries. Try making your own favorite pastry for the shell or buy a frozen one. Just check the frozen pie shell package and pick one with natural ingredients. This is a rich recipe, so you probably won't want to eat it every day, but it is a great dish for a special occasion.

Serves 6

ingredients

flour for rolling out pastry

1 favorite recipe pie crust or 1 frozen 9-inch pie shell

6 slices thick-cut smoked bacon (4 ounces, or ¾ cup chopped)

4 eggs

1½ cups heavy cream, or 1 cup whole milk and ½ cup heavy cream combined

freshly ground black pepper to taste

On your mark, get set . . .

- Preheat the oven to 375°F.

- If using your own pie shell: Lightly flour a clean work surface. Sprinkle a little flour on a rolling pin and roll it back and forth a few times to completely cover it with flour. Lay the chilled pastry on the work surface and sprinkle the top lightly with flour.

- Lay the rolling pin in the center of the pastry and gently but firmly roll the pin back and forth to flatten it. Now start rolling out the pastry, always starting from the center and rolling just to the edges of the pastry. Pick the pastry up and give it a slight turn. Repeat these steps until the pastry is about ⅛ inch thick and a few inches larger than a 9-inch pie dish.

- Place the rolling pin on top of the farthest edge of the pastry. Bring the edge up and over the rolling pin. Roll the rest of the pastry onto the rolling pin. Lift the rolling pin and place it over the center of the pie dish.

- Unroll the pastry and let it sink into the shape of the dish. Try not to stretch it. Leave at least 1 inch of pastry overhanging the edge, then cut away the excess pastry.

- To make a decorative edge, roll over the edge of the pastry and gently press your finger into it to give it a slightly curved shape. Repeat this all around the edge.

- Chill the shell while you prepare the other ingredients.

- If using a frozen pie shell: Follow the package directions for the best results.

Cook!

- Cut the bacon into small strips about 1 inch wide and 1/4 inch thick.

- Cook the bacon in a 10-inch skillet on medium heat until it starts to turn brown and slightly crisp. Drain the bacon on paper towels and set aside.

- Beat together the eggs and cream, or milk and cream combination, with a whisk or electric hand mixer until frothy. This is called the custard. Add the pepper.

- Remove the pie shell from the refrigerator and place it on a baking sheet.

- Press the bacon pieces gently into the bottom of the shell.

- Pour the custard over the top, being careful not to fill the shell more than three-quarters full.

- Place the quiche on the middle rack of the oven and bake for 30 to 35 minutes. The quiche will puff up and turn golden brown.

- Let it rest for 10 minutes before slicing and serving.

salads

Combination Salad *Salade Niçoise*

This famous salad is from Nice, located in the south of France on the Mediterranean shore. The ingredients are dressed separately with a Dijon mustard dressing. Look for the freshest ingredients when shopping for this salad, and serve it with French bread for a great summertime lunch or supper. To make this salad vegetarian, simply omit the tuna.

Serves 6

ingredients

dressing
½ cup extra-virgin olive oil
1 tablespoon red wine vinegar
1 tablespoon fresh lemon juice
1 tablespoon Dijon mustard
1 tablespoon chopped fresh flat-leaf parsley or fresh chives
¼ teaspoon dry mustard
freshly ground black pepper to taste

salad
1 head Boston lettuce
8 to 10 red-skin, Yukon gold, or other small potatoes (golf-ball size)
½ pound fresh green beans
6 to 8 Niçoise or pitted black olives
2 ripe tomatoes
3 eggs
1 can (6 ounces) oil-packed tuna

On your mark, get set . . .

- Place all the ingredients for the dressing in a glass jar with a lid and shake well to combine. Set aside.

- Wash the lettuce leaves and pat or spin dry. Wrap the lettuce in paper towels to absorb any excess water and refrigerate.

- Rinse and scrub the potatoes to remove any dirt.

- Rinse the green beans. Snap off the stem end of each bean and pull it down to remove any string.

- Count the olives and set aside.

- Wash the tomatoes and remove the stem ends. Cut the tomatoes into quarters.

Cook!

- Bring a 3-quart pan of salted water to a boil. Drop in the green beans and cook for 5 to 6 minutes, or until tender but still a little crunchy when you bite one.

- Drain the beans and flood with cold running water to stop the cooking. Cut the beans in half and set aside.

- Place the eggs in a small pan of water and bring to a boil. Reduce the heat to simmer and cook for 12 minutes.

- In the meantime, prepare the potatoes: Bring a 3-quart pan of salted water to a boil. Add the potatoes and cook for 10 to 12 minutes, or until they feel tender when pierced with the tip of a knife.

- Drain the potatoes and return them to the pan for 1 or 2 minutes to absorb any excess cooking liquid. Remove the potatoes from the heat and set aside to cool.

- When the eggs have finished cooking, place the pan in the sink and flood the eggs with cold running water for 1 minute. Allow the eggs to cool in the cold water.

- Peel the eggs under gently running cold water. Set the eggs aside.

- Once the potatoes are cool enough to handle, slice them into 1/4-inch slices.

- Place the potatoes, green beans, tomatoes, and 1 1/2 tablespoons of the dressing in a large bowl; remember to shake the dressing again before measuring. Toss well. Set the vegetables aside for 15 minutes to allow them to absorb the dressing.

- Arrange the lettuce leaves on a serving platter.

- Place the marinated potatoes, green beans, and tomatoes in the center of the lettuce.

- Drain the tuna, flake it with a fork, and place it around the potatoes. Drizzle the remaining dressing over the salad.

- Cut the eggs into quarters and set the eggs and olives around the edge of the platter.

- Serve accompanied with French Bread for a complete summer meal.

(See pages 38-39 for photo.)

YOU MAY REMOVE THE PITS FROM THE NIÇOISE OLIVES BEFORE SERVING THEM, BUT IT WILL BE EASIER TO SIMPLY REMIND YOUR GUESTS THAT THE OLIVES HAVE PITS AND TO NIBBLE AROUND THEM.

Mixed Salad *Insalata Mista*

The Italians have been making salads for a very long time, and that's why they are so good at it. This recipe uses a homemade dressing that will make you think differently about the ones that come prepared in a bottle. Look for the freshest greens you can find. You can be creative with the salad ingredients or follow this recipe. The carrots, sweet red pepper, and celery should be firm and the tomatoes ripe. Remember, the freshest ingredients make the best salads.

Serves 8

ingredients

Salad
1 small head romaine lettuce
1 head Boston lettuce
½ bunch fresh spinach (about 6 ounces)
1 small head radicchio
½ sweet red pepper
2 small carrots
2 stalks celery hearts
2 ripe tomatoes
salt and freshly ground pepper to taste

Dressing
⅓ cup extra virgin olive oil
1 tablespoon red wine vinegar
1 teaspoon salt
¼ teaspoon sugar
1 clove garlic, crushed
1 teaspoon fresh lemon juice
¼ teaspoon freshly ground pepper

On your mark...

- Fill a clean sink with fresh cold water.

- Separate the leaves of the romaine lettuce, the Boston lettuce, the spinach, and the radicchio, and drop them into the water. Let them soak for a few minutes, gently moving them around with your hands to help dislodge any dirt.

- Remove the leaves and place them in a colander. Drain the water from the sink and clean any dirt or sand from the bottom.

- Refill the sink and repeat the washing at least once.

- Use a salad spinner to dry the greens. If you don't have a spinner, lay paper toweling on a clean countertop and place the greens on it. Gently roll up the leaves in the paper towels to absorb the extra moisture. You may have to do this in two batches. You can refrigerate the greens still rolled in the paper towels or use them immediately.

Get set...

- Wash and seed the red pepper, and cut into thin slices.

- Wash and peel the carrots, and cut into thin slices.

- Wash the celery hearts and cut into thin slices.

- Wash the tomatoes and cut into wedges.

- To assemble the salad, tear all the greens into bite-size pieces—do not cut them—and place them in a large serving bowl. Add the rest of the salad ingredients. Mix well to combine. Cover with a clean damp cloth and chill until ready to serve.

- For the dressing, combine all the ingredients in a glass jar with a lid, and shake.

Toss!

- When you are ready to serve the salad, remove the garlic clove from the dressing.

- Give the jar another shake and pour the dressing over the salad.

- Add salt and pepper to taste and toss well.

chef's tip TOSS THE SALAD WITH THE DRESSING JUST BEFORE YOU SERVE IT. THAT WAY YOU'LL BE SURE EVERYTHING IS FRESH AND CRISP.

Tomato Salad *Insalata di Pomodoro*

There are few foods in the world that combine as well as fresh tomatoes and fresh basil. They just say "summer" when you taste them together. Try this recipe when tomatoes are in season, or when you can find ripe ones with a rich red color in the market. This classic Italian salad is popular in Sardinia, where the tomatoes are so flavorful.

Serves 4

ingredients

3 medium-size ripe tomatoes
1 medium-size red onion
⅓ cup extra virgin olive oil
½ teaspoon salt

¼ teaspoon freshly ground
  pepper
5 or 6 fresh basil leaves
1 tablespoon cold water

On your mark, get set, toss!

- Wash the tomatoes and set them on a cutting board. Cut out the stem circle at the top of each tomato and discard. Cut the tomatoes into small wedges and place them in a bowl.

- Peel the red onion and cut into thin slices, then mix in with the tomatoes.

- Add the olive oil, salt, and pepper. Mix well.

- Wash the basil leaves and tear into small pieces. Add to the salad, along with the 1 tablespoon cold water.

- Toss well. Don't refrigerate or the tomatoes will lose their flavor.

pasta, pizza, and polenta

Everyone loves pasta!

Pasta is the food of the future. Pasta is also the food of the past. This simple and amazing staple of the Italian kitchen has been a favorite across Italy and throughout the world for centuries. It will probably remain so for many more centuries to come.

Since pasta is made with just two basic ingredients, flour and water, nobody can agree on when or where it was first created. There is an old theory that the Venetian traveler Marco Polo brought it back to Italy from China in the thirteenth century. Many food historians, however, now believe that pasta was already being made in Italy years before Marco Polo's travels. There is another theory that pasta was made thousands of years ago on the islands of Sicily and Sardinia, where wheat was commonly grown.

No matter what theory you believe, one thing is certain: pasta is loved everywhere because it is a nearly perfect food.

Pasta is packed with nutrients and vitamins B_1 and B_2. Even better news is that in four ounces of cooked dried pasta there are only 325 calories. Fresh pasta has 365 calories in four ounces. So it is not true, as some people believe, that pasta makes you fat as long as you don't load it with carbo-rich sauces.

When shopping for pasta, be creative. You don't have to buy just spaghetti. Believe it or not, there are more than three hundred varieties of pasta, in all shapes and sizes, from which to choose. Pasta is sold in two ways: dried and fresh. Fresh, or *pasta fresca*, is made with flour and water, usually mixed with eggs. It needs to be used fairly soon after you buy it. Dried pasta, or *pasta asciutta*, is a mixture of flour and water that is dried before being sold. It can be stored for a long time.

How to Cook Pasta

- Begin with a big pot. It should be deep. Pasta loves plenty of water to move around in as it cooks. That way it will cook evenly and won't stick together.

- Add salt to the cold water, about 1/2 teaspoon for every quart of water.

- Cover the pot and bring the water to a full rolling boil.

- Remove the cover.

- Add the pasta and return the water to a boil. Cook uncovered.

- Check the package instructions for the exact length of cooking time. Set a timer.

- Every so often stir the pasta. If necessary, lower the temperature so the water does not boil too fast. The water should boil fast enough to keep the pasta moving, but not so fast that it boils over.

- When the pasta is cooked, ask your adult assistant to help you strain it through a colander in the sink.

- Never rinse the pasta.

   Your pasta is now ready for the sauce. There are two ways you can serve pasta. One way is in a large bowl, family style. The other way is in individual bowls or on plates. The first step is always the same, no matter how you serve it. Place the drained pasta in a large bowl. Add a cup or so of the sauce and toss well to coat the strands. For family style, add more sauce on top and serve. For individual servings, place a single portion of sauced pasta on each plate, top with extra sauce, and serve. You can pass more sauce at the table but remember, the Italians never put on a lot of sauce, because they want to taste the pasta, too.

There is a world of pasta to choose from out there.

Tomato Sauce *Sugo di Pomodoro*

Here is a simple recipe for tomato sauce that you can use not only with your favorite pasta, but as a topping for pizza, too. It is perfect to make in the summer, when tomatoes are at their peak of flavor. You can make it any time of the year, though, using canned Italian tomatoes, which work just as well as the fresh. Try adding cooked chicken, fresh vegetables, or seafood to the sauce. This recipe makes about 3 cups, enough for 1 pound of cooked pasta.

Serves 4

ingredients

2 pounds ripe tomatoes or 1 can (28 ounces) chopped Italian tomatoes

1 medium-size red or yellow onion

2 cloves garlic

¼ cup fresh basil leaves (optional)

¼ cup extra virgin olive oil

2 teaspoons dried oregano

1 teaspoon sugar

2 teaspoons salt

freshly ground pepper to taste

On your mark, get set . . .

- Wash the tomatoes and set them on a cutting board. Cut out the stem circle at the top of each tomato and discard. Chop the tomatoes and place in a bowl.

- Peel and chop the onion and garlic. You are making what the Italians call a *battuto.*

- If using fresh basil, wash the leaves to remove any dirt and tear into small pieces.

Cook!

- Place a 4-quart saucepan over low heat and add the olive oil, onion, and garlic.

- Sauté for 4 to 5 minutes, or until the onion and garlic turn golden. This is the *soffritto.* Be careful not to burn it. If you do, you must discard the ingredients and start over, or your finished sauce will have a bitter taste.

- Add the tomatoes, basil, oregano, sugar, salt, and pepper.

- Continue to cook for 20 to 30 minutes, stirring occasionally. The sauce is ready when the color has softened and the flavor is sweet and creamy.

chef's tip

TRY ADDING 1 POUND OF FRESH SHRIMP TO THE SAUCE. WASH, PEEL, AND REMOVE THE VEIN FROM THE SHRIMP. WHEN THE SAUCE IS READY, ADD THE SHRIMP TO THE SAUCEPAN, COOKING JUST UNTIL IT TURNS PINK (ABOUT 2 MINUTES). TOSS WITH COOKED PASTA. THIS SAUCE IS ALSO PERFECT OVER POLENTA.

Pasta with Spring Vegetables

Pasta alla Primavera con Asparagi e Cipolle

The Italians have a way with vegetables. Not only do they grow some of the most perfect vegetables in the world, they also are experts at preparing them. Here is a recipe from Florence that combines a few simple vegetables into an exciting and flavorful pasta sauce. This style of preparing vegetables dates back to a Renaissance cooking technique. After you taste this dish, you will understand why it is still being prepared today.

Serves 6

ingredients

1 small red onion
1 clove garlic
1 stalk celery
1 medium-size carrot
½ pound Swiss chard
1 pound fresh asparagus
1 pound fresh tomatoes
1 medium-size zucchini
3 tablespoons extra virgin olive oil
2 teaspoons salt

freshly ground pepper to taste
½ cup homemade Vegetable or Chicken Broth, pages 16 and 12, or canned low-sodium
5 or 6 fresh basil leaves, torn into small pieces
½ teaspoon dried oregano
salt for cooking pasta
1 pound dried spaghetti or linguine

On your mark, get set . . .

- Peel the red onion and chop into small pieces.

- Crush, peel and chop the garlic.

- Wash and scrub the outside skins of the celery and carrot, and chop into small pieces.

- Wash the Swiss chard stalks and cut into 1/2-inch pieces, and cut or tear the leaves into thin slices.

- Rinse the asparagus with cold water and cut into 1-inch pieces.

- Wash the tomatoes and cut into small chunks.

- Wash the zucchini and cut into chunks.

Cook!

- Heat the olive oil in a 12-inch skillet over low heat. Add the red onion, garlic, celery, and carrot, and sauté for 10 minutes.

- Add the Swiss chard, asparagus, tomatoes, zucchini, 2 teaspoons salt, and pepper, and carefully mix together all the ingredients.

- Add the vegetable or chicken broth, torn basil leaves, and oregano. Cook for 30 minutes on low heat or a gentle simmer.

- While the sauce is cooking, bring a large pot of cold salted water to a boil. Cook the spaghetti according to the package directions.

- When the spaghetti is *al dente*,* have your adult assistant help you strain it through a colander. Pour the spaghetti into a large serving bowl.

- Spoon one ladle of the hot sauce over the spaghetti and mix well, coating all the strands with the sauce.

- Pour the rest of the sauce over the top, toss together, and serve immediately.

Al dente literally means "to the tooth." It means the pasta is just a little hard and chewy, not very soft. That is the way Italians usually like to eat their pasta.

Spaghetti and Meatballs

Spaghetti con Polpette di Carne

Is there any dish more loved than spaghetti and meatballs? This classic recipe comes from Naples. The sauce has a real old-fashioned, slow-cooked flavor. Once you taste your homemade sauce and meatballs, you will want to make this dish again and again.

Serves 4 to 6

ingredients

Meatballs

½ pound sweet Italian sausage (3 links)
½ pound ground round beef
2 eggs, lightly beaten
½ cup plain bread crumbs
2 tablespoons chopped Italian flat-leaf parsley
1 tablespoon chopped yellow onion
½ cup freshly grated Parmesan cheese
1 clove garlic, crushed, peeled, and chopped
¼ teaspoon grated nutmeg (optional)
½ tablespoon salt
4 tablespoons extra virgin olive oil for frying

Sauce

2 cloves garlic
1 can (5.5 ounces) tomato paste
2 cans (28 ounces) chopped tomatoes
1 medium-size yellow onion
¼ cup extra virgin olive oil
2 cups homemade Chicken Broth, page 12, or canned low-sodium
½ tablespoon dried oregano
½ tablespoon salt
freshly ground pepper to taste

1 pound dried spaghetti
salt for cooking pasta

On your mark . . .

- For the meatballs: Remove the casing from the sausage links. To do this, place 1 sausage on a cutting board and make a slit in the casing the length of the sausage with the tip of a sharp knife. Peel away the casing and discard.

- Using the flat side of the knife, spread the sausage meat onto the surface of the cutting board, then chop it to break up the meat into small pieces.

- Repeat with the other links. Wash the cutting board.

- In a large bowl mix together all the ingredients for the meatballs, except the olive oil. If using your hands to do the mixing, make sure they are very clean. Refrigerate the meatball mixture.

- For the sauce: Crush, peel, and chop the garlic. Open the cans of tomato paste and tomatoes. Peel the onion and chop into small pieces.

Get set . . .

- Heat ¼ cup extra virgin olive oil in a 10-inch skillet over low heat. Add the garlic and cook slowly for 1 minute. If the garlic begins to brown, lower the heat.

- Add the onion and cook slowly for 5 to 6 minutes, or until it changes from white to almost clear.

Cook!

- Place a large pot (8-quart) on the stove and add the cooked garlic and onion. Turn the heat to medium. Cook for 1 minute.

- Raise the heat to medium-high and add the tomato paste. Cook for 1 to 2 minutes, using a long-handled spoon to gently stir the mixture. Be careful not to splash yourself.

- Add the chicken broth and cook for another 5 minutes, stirring occasionally.

- Add the chopped tomatoes and bring to a boil. This will take about 10 minutes.

- When the sauce starts to boil, reduce the heat to medium and cook for 30 minutes, stirring occasionally. Use a large metal spoon to skim off the light-colored foam that rises to the top of the pot.

- Add the oregano, salt, and pepper.

- While the sauce is cooking, you can shape and brown the meatballs. Wash your hands. Scoop up a tablespoon of the meat mixture and roll it between the palms of your hands to shape it into a ball about 1 1/2 inches wide. For 6 servings make the meatballs 1 inch wide. If the mixture is too wet, add more bread crumbs. Place the meatballs on a tray as you form them.

- Heat a 10-inch skillet over medium-low heat and add 2 tablespoons of the olive oil. Brown the meatballs in the skillet, 4 at a time, using tongs to turn them as they brown. Add the remaining 2 tablespoons olive oil to the skillet as needed, to keep the meatballs from sticking. Place the meatballs on a plate.

- After the sauce has cooked for 30 minutes, add the meatballs to the pot and cook on medium heat for another 45 minutes.

- Cook the spaghetti in a large pot of salted water according to the package directions.

- With the help of your adult assistant, strain the spaghetti in a colander and place in a large serving bowl.

- Add about 1 cup of the sauce and toss to coat the strands.

- Serve the spaghetti on individual plates, spooning additional sauce on each and topping with 2 or 3 meatballs.

Pasta Sauce from Bologna
Ragù alla Bolognese

Here is a truly classic Italian recipe. This sauce from the northern city of Bologna may be the most famous of all Italian pasta sauces. It is so famous that nearly every Bolognese will have his or her own version of just how it should be made. There is even the "official" recipe that hangs in Bologna's city hall. Don't be put off by the long cooking time. The slow cooking of this ragù produces its great flavor. This sauce is even better the day after you make it, but who can wait a day to eat it?

Serves 4 to 6

ingredients

1 stalk celery
1 carrot
1 medium-size onion
1 can (28 ounces) crushed tomatoes
2 slices bacon (2 to 3 ounces)
3 links sweet Italian sausage (½ pound)
3 tablespoons butter
2 tablespoons extra virgin olive oil
½ pound ground beef chuck
1 teaspoon salt

1 cup homemade Chicken Broth, page 12, or canned low-sodium
2 tablespoons tomato paste
¼ teaspoon ground nutmeg (optional)
½ cup whole milk
freshly ground pepper to taste
salt for cooking pasta
1 pound dried pappardella or penne pasta
freshly grated Parmigiano-Reggiano cheese for serving

On your mark . . .

- Wash and finely chop the celery and carrot. Measure ½ cup each.

- Peel and chop the onion and measure 3/4 cup.

- Open the canned tomatoes.

Get Set . . .

- Chop the bacon into small chunks, all about the same size.

- Remove the casing from the sausage links. To do this, place 1 sausage on a cutting board and make a slit in the casing the length of the sausage with the tip of a sharp knife. Peel away the casing and discard.

- Using the flat side of the knife, spread the sausage meat onto the surface of the cutting board, then chop it to break up the meat into small pieces.

- Repeat with the other links. Wash the cutting board.

Cook!

- Place a 6-quart pot over low heat and add the butter, olive oil, and onion. Cook for 2 to 3 minutes.

- Add the celery and carrot and cook for another 2 to 3 minutes.

- Add the bacon and cook for 1 minute.

- Raise the heat to medium. Add the ground beef, sausage meat, and 1 teaspoon salt. Cook until the meat has lost its red color, about 3 to 4 minutes. Add 1/2 cup of the chicken broth and cook for 3 to 4 minutes.

- Add the tomatoes, tomato paste, nutmeg, milk, and pepper.

- Add the remaining 1/2 cup chicken broth.

- When the sauce starts to bubble, reduce the heat to simmer. Cook slowly for at least 1 to 1 1/2 hours. Stir occasionally.

- About 30 minutes into the cooking, skim off the oil that rises to the top and discard it.

- About 20 minutes before the sauce is done, boil a large pot of salted water and cook the pasta according to the package directions.

- Strain the pasta with the help of your adult assistant and place in a serving bowl. Toss with a small amount of the sauce to coat the strands.

- Spoon the rest of the sauce over the pasta and serve with grated Parmigiano-Reggiano cheese on the side.

Swordfish Pasta, Sicilian Style

Pasta con Pescespada alla Siciliana

The island of Sicily is rich with exotic flavors and local specialties. Here's a classic fresh fish recipe that is still served in the port city of Palermo. Sicilians are outstanding seafood cooks, because there is such a great variety of fish available from the three seas that surround their beautiful island. Look for the freshest boneless fish steaks you can find when preparing this dish. If swordfish is not available, you can substitute tuna, red snapper, or salmon.

Serves 6

ingredients

4 fresh boneless swordfish steaks (about 28 to 32 ounces total)
1 small onion (about ¾ cup chopped)
2 cloves garlic
1 stalk celery
¼ cup currants or raisins
⅛ cup pine nuts or chopped walnuts
2 teaspoons salt
freshly ground pepper to taste

1 pound fresh tomatoes (about 2 cups chopped)
8 to 10 fresh basil leaves
½ cup pitted green or black olives
1 tablespoon capers
1 fresh orange
salt for cooking pasta
1 pound dried penne pasta or spaghetti
3 tablespoons extra virgin olive oil

On your mark, get set . . .

- Wash the fish steaks under cold water and pat dry. If there is any skin on the fish steaks, remove it.

- Cut the fish into 2-inch cubes, place in a bowl, and refrigerate until ready to use. Wash the cutting board.

- Peel and chop the onion and measure 3/4 cup.

- Crush, peel, and chop the garlic.

- Wash and chop the celery, measure 3/4 cup, and set aside.

- Measure the currants, nuts, and salt. Place these ingredients and the pepper close to the onion, garlic, and celery, but don't combine.

- Wash the tomatoes. Cut out the stem circle at the top of each tomato and discard. Chop into small chunks, measure 2 cups, and place in a medium-size bowl.

- Wash and tear the basil leaves into small pieces and add to the tomatoes.

- Chop the olives into small pieces and add to the bowl.

- Rinse the capers in a small hand strainer and add those as well.

- Squeeze the juice from the orange, removing any pits, and add to the bowl.

- Stir together until well combined.

Cook!

- Bring a large pot (6- to 8-quart) of cold salted water to boil for the pasta. Cook the pasta according to the package directions.

- In the meantime, heat the olive oil in a skillet (10- to 12-inch) over low heat. Add the onion, garlic, celery, currants, nuts, salt, and pepper. Cook for 3 to 4 minutes.

- Raise the heat to medium and add the tomato mixture to the skillet. Cook for 10 minutes.

- Reduce the heat to low and add the fish cubes. Mix well with a spoon to make sure all the ingredients are combined.

- Add about 1/2 cup of the pasta cooking water to the skillet. Cook for 10 to 15 minutes, or until the fish is tender.

- Get your adult assistant to help you strain the pasta in a colander.

- Pour the pasta into a serving bowl and add the fish and sauce. Toss together gently, and the dish is ready to serve.

Pizza Dough *La Pasta da Pizza*

Here is a recipe for a perfect pizza dough that can also make a perfect bread. When preparing any recipe with flour and yeast, it is important to have extra flour close by. You will need to sprinkle it on the work surface when you knead the dough. You may also need a tablespoon or so more than the recipe calls for. Lots of things, such as humidity, altitude, and the age of the flour, can affect how much flour you'll need for the dough. This recipe makes two 10-inch pizzas or one large loaf of bread.

ingredients

1¼ cups warm water
  (100°F-110°F)
1 package (¼ ounce) active
  dry yeast
3 level cups unbleached
  all-purpose flour

½ level tablespoon salt
1 tablespoon extra virgin olive oil
extra flour for kneading
extra olive oil for the bowl

On your mark . . .

- Measure 1/4 cup of the warm water into a small bowl. Make sure the water is not too hot, which will stop the yeast from becoming active, or too cool, which will keep it from starting. Use a kitchen thermometer or run the water over your fingers for a few seconds to make sure it is just warm.

- Sprinkle the package of yeast over the water, give it a stir, and then cover it.

- The water and yeast combination will need 10 minutes to become active. You will know the yeast is active if after 10 minutes soft bubbles appear on the surface of the water. If the bubbles do not appear, you'll need to start over with a new package of yeast and fresh water.

Get Set . . .

- Place 3 cups flour in a large bowl and sprinkle the salt over the flour.

- With a spoon make a well in the center of the flour. Pour the active yeast and water into the well. Mix with a fork until a wet paste forms.

- Combine the remaining 1 cup warm water and 1 tablespoon olive oil. Pour into the bowl and mix all the ingredients together. You should now have a soft dough.

- Sprinkle a tablespoon of flour on a clean work surface. Sprinkle extra flour on your hands to keep the dough from sticking to them. Remove the dough from the bowl and place it on the work surface.

- Begin kneading by pressing the dough away from you with the palms of your hands and then folding it in half. Pick it up and give it a turn to the right or left. Work the dough over and over for 5 to 6 minutes, repeating that same action. Be sure to keep turning the dough in the same direction. It will be sticky in the beginning, but don't worry.

- From time to time, give the dough a few punches to get the air out. Knead until it is smooth and springy. Now it is ready for a rest.

- Drizzle a small amount of olive oil into a clean bowl and place the dough on top of it. Give the ball of dough a few spins and turn it over to lightly coat it with the oil.

- Cover with a sheet of plastic wrap and a couple of heavy, clean kitchen towels.

- Place the dough in a warm, draft-free spot where it can rise undisturbed for 1 1/2 hours, or until it doubles in size.

Cook!

- To make the dough into pizza, follow the recipe on page 62.

- To make the dough into bread: Sprinkle a little flour on your hands. Pull the dough out of the bowl and punch it down to remove air. Knead again for 4 to 6 minutes on a lightly floured work surface.

- Shape the dough to fit into a lightly oiled 8 1/2 x 4 1/2-inch bread pan. Brush the top with a little olive oil.

- Cover with plastic wrap or wax paper and heavy, clean kitchen towels. Let the bread rise again in a warm, draft-free spot for 1 hour.

- Preheat the oven to 375°F.

- Bake for 50 to 60 minutes.

- Remove the bread from the oven and let it cool for a few minutes. Using clean hot pads, carefully tip the pan over and remove the bread. The bread will make a hollow sound when you tap it and that means it's done. If it's not done, return it to the bread pan and bake another 5 to 10 minutes.

Pizza from Naples *Pizza Napoletana*

Everybody loves pizza! It is simply one of the most popular foods on the planet today. There are as many varieties of pizza and toppings as the imagination will allow. Why not try making pizza at home? It's fun to make and even more fun to eat. This simple version from Naples, made with a few delicious toppings, will have you saying, "Homemade is best!"

Serves 4

ingredients

1½ cups canned chopped Italian tomatoes
½ pound mozzarella cheese
1 tablespoon extra virgin olive oil

2 teaspoons dried oregano
8 anchovy fillets (optional)
extra olive oil for the pan
1 recipe Pizza Dough (page 60)
freshly ground pepper to taste

On your mark . . .

- Preheat the oven to 450°F.

- Drain the tomatoes in a hand strainer and shake off any excess liquid.

- Grate the mozzarella into a bowl, using the large holes of a cheese grater.

- Add the olive oil to the cheese and toss.

- Measure the oregano into a small bowl.

- If using the anchovies, drain off any excess oil and separate the fillets on a plate. Tear the fillets into small pieces.

- Lightly oil an 11 x 16-inch baking pan or cookie sheet.

Get Set . . .

- If making one large pizza, keep the dough in one piece. If making two smaller pizzas, divide the dough and the topping ingredients in half. Cover one half of the dough as you prepare the other half.

- Place the dough on the baking pan and, using your fingers and the palms of your hands, press and push the dough to stretch it to cover the pan. Try not to tear it. If you do tear the dough, simply give it a pinch at the torn spot to repair it. Don't worry if the shape is not exact. Remember, your pizza is made by hand, so it should not have a perfect shape.

- After you get the dough about 1/4 inch thick, use your fingers to make lots of tiny dents all across the surface.

- Top with the tomatoes, spreading them across the dough. Then add the mozzarella.

- If using the anchovies, press them into the dough.

- Sprinkle with the oregano and a little pepper. The pizza is ready to bake.

Cook!

- Bake for 25 to 30 minutes, or until the crust is brown and crispy at the edges.

- Slice and serve hot.

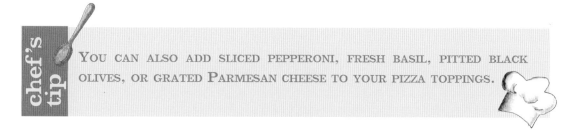

chef's tip

YOU CAN ALSO ADD SLICED PEPPERONI, FRESH BASIL, PITTED BLACK OLIVES, OR GRATED PARMESAN CHEESE TO YOUR PIZZA TOPPINGS.

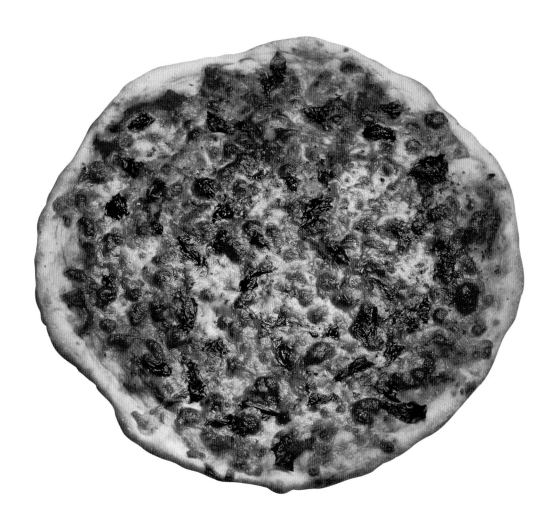

Instant Polenta *Polenta Veloce*

If you really want to experience northern Italian cooking, you must try polenta. Polenta is made from specially ground corn, and it requires a long, slow cooking time. Instant polenta cooks in much less time. Once you discover how many great meals you can create with polenta, you will know why it is such a popular part of Italian cooking. Follow the suggestions at the end of the recipe for even more ideas for cooking with polenta.

Serves 6

ingredients

6 ½ cups water
½ tablespoon salt

2 tablespoons extra virgin olive oil
2 cups Italian instant polenta

On your mark, get set, cook!

- Bring the water, salt, and olive oil to a full boil in a nonstick 6-quart pan.

- Rinse a 10-inch square glass baking pan with cold water, but don't dry it. Keep it ready next to the stove.

- When the liquid boils, remove the pan from the stove. Pour the polenta into the boiling liquid in a thin, steady stream and stir with a wooden spoon or a whisk. Be alert that you don't splash yourself with the polenta as it cooks.

- Return the pan to the stove, cover, and cook for 12 to 15 minutes on low heat. Stir the polenta for another minute after the cooking time has finished.

- Pour the polenta into the wet baking pan. Smooth the surface of the hot polenta with a spoon or rubber spatula so that it is all the same thickness.

- Allow the polenta to cool and become firm. The polenta can be cut into 1/2-inch-thick slices and used in Polenta Pie with Sausage and Cheese (page 65).

- Wrap any leftover polenta, refrigerate, and use within 1 week.

Other serving suggestions

When the polenta has finished cooking in the pan on the stove, add 3 tablespoons butter and 1/2 cup freshly grated Parmigiano-Reggiano cheese. Mix well and serve immediately.

Fry polenta slices in 1 tablespoon olive oil and 1 tablespoon butter combined. Brown the slices for about 3 to 4 minutes on each side, turning carefully with a spatula. Serve as a side dish or top with your favorite pasta sauce and grated cheese.

chef's tip

CLEANING THE POLENTA PAN CAN LOOK LIKE AN IMPOSSIBLE JOB, BUT HERE'S A TIP TO MAKE IT EASIER. FILL THE PAN WITH COLD WATER AND LET IT SOAK WHILE YOU ARE ENJOYING YOUR MEAL. BY THE TIME YOU HAVE FINISHED, CLEANUP SHOULD BE A SNAP!

Polenta Pie with Sausage and Cheese
Polenta al Forno con Salsicce

Winters in the Piedmont region of northern Italy can be cold. A hearty dish like this polenta pie is just the thing to keep the chill out. Polenta is also a great way to use leftover pasta sauces. This recipe is excellent when you have a lot of friends over for dinner. It can easily be doubled to make two pies. You choose the pasta sauce you like best to go into the filling of this layered pie.

Serves 6

ingredients

Pie shell

1 recipe Instant Polenta (page 64),
  cooked and cooled

Filling

1 pound sweet Italian sausage
  (6 links)
1 medium-size yellow onion
4 ounces fontina cheese
4 ounces mozzarella cheese

2 ounces Parmesan cheese
½ cup homemade or bottled
  pasta sauce
2 teaspoons extra virgin olive oil

On your mark, get set . . .

- Prepare the Instant Polenta. Cool until firm and cut into 1/2-inch-thick slices. Set aside.

- Remove the casings from the Italian sausage: Place 1 link on a cutting board and, with the tip of a sharp knife, make a cut along the length of the sausage. The meat will separate from the casing. Peel away the casing and discard.

- Using the flat side of the knife, spread the sausage meat onto the surface of the cutting board, then chop it to break up the meat into small pieces.

- Repeat with the other links. Wash the cutting board.

- Peel and chop the onion.

- Grate the fontina and mozzarella cheeses, using the large holes of a cheese grater, and combine in a bowl.

- Grate the Parmesan cheese, using the smallest holes, and set aside.

- Measure out the pasta sauce and set aside.

Cook!

- Preheat the oven to 400°F.

- Heat the olive oil in a 10-inch skillet over low heat. Add the onion and cook for 3 to 4 minutes.

- Add the sausage meat and cook for 5 to 6 minutes, or until the meat has lost its red color.

- Remove the sausage and onion from the pan with a slotted spoon to a clean bowl and set aside.

- To assemble the pie: Arrange some of the polenta slices so that they completely cover the bottom and sides of a 10-inch square baking pan or cast-iron skillet.

- Sprinkle 1/4 cup of the fontina and mozzarella cheese mixture evenly across the bottom layer of polenta. Top with the sausage and onion.

- Spoon on the pasta sauce, then sprinkle on the rest of the fontina and mozzarella.

- Use the remaining polenta slices to form the top layer of the pie. The total amount of polenta you use will vary depending on the size of your pan, so don't worry if you have leftover polenta.

- Sprinkle the grated cheese over the top.

- Bake for 35 to 40 minutes. Cut into slices and serve hot.

chef's tip

TO MAKE THE PIE AHEAD OF TIME, FOLLOW THE RECIPE TO PREPARE ALL THE INGREDIENTS, AND LET THEM CHILL COMPLETELY IN THE REFRIGERATOR BEFORE YOU ASSEMBLE THEM INTO THE PIE. ONCE THE PIE IS ASSEMBLED, YOU CAN REFRIGERATE IT FOR UP TO 3 HOURS. INCREASE THE BAKING TIME BY 10 TO 15 MINUTES.

a taco party

A Taco Party *Taquisa*

It's time for a *taquisa*—a taco party! It's just the right way to show off a few of your Mexican recipes and celebrate a special occasion at the same time. You can do most of the preparation ahead of time, and the ingredients for tacos are easy to make and fun to eat. Forget about buying those boxed tortilla shells from the supermarket. Instead, make your own crispy or soft tortillas. Your guests will enjoy putting together their own tacos, and you will be able to join the fun. To add an authentic touch to your party, don't forget to have plenty of Refried Beans (page 90) and White Rice (page 85) on hand.

Serves 6

ingredients

1 small head romaine or iceberg lettuce
1 pound Mexican queso blanco,
    Monterey Jack, or Cheddar cheese
24 corn tortillas
    (See page 162)
½ cup canola or corn oil for
    frying tortillas

Taco fillings (prepare at least 2)
1 recipe Chicken Breasts in Stock
    (page 84)
1 recipe Little Pork (page 82)
1 recipe Ground Meat Filling for
    Tortillas (page 80)
1 recipe Guacamole (page 78)

Salsa (prepare at least 1)
1 recipe Mexican Sauce (page 73)
1 recipe Green Salsa (page 74)

On your mark, get set . . .

- Remove any brown or dark leaves from the lettuce. Cut off the stem end and discard.

- Wash the lettuce under cold running water to remove any dirt. Drain to remove excess water.

- Cut the lettuce in half lengthwise and then cut crosswise into thin strips. Refrigerate the lettuce.

- Grate the cheese and put in a serving bowl.

- Place the tortillas on a plate. Measure the oil and set aside.

- Select the taco fillings from the list. A good rule to follow is that each guest will probably want about 1/4 cup filling for each taco he or she makes.

- The salsa, lettuce, and cheese can be at room temperature or cold. The meat fillings should be hot. If you are serving Refried Beans and White Rice, they should also be served hot. The tortillas should be served warm.

Cook!

To make crispy tortillas:

- Preheat the oven to 200°F.

- Line a metal baking sheet with paper towels and place it in the oven. Be careful not to place the paper towels near the heating element.

- Line a second, smaller metal tray with paper towels and place it next to the stove.

- Heat a frying pan with 2 tablespoons of the oil on medium heat.

- Fry the tortillas, one at a time, for about 1 1/2 minutes on each side, turning them with a pair of tongs.

- Remove each tortilla as it starts to get crispy and to brown slightly.

- Lay the hot tortilla on the tray next to the stove and, still using the tongs, fold it in half. After a minute or two, place the crispy tortillas on the baking sheet in the oven to keep warm.

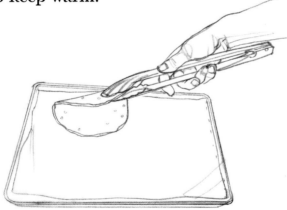

- Repeat this step, adding more oil to the pan as needed, until you have made all the tortillas into crispy shells.

To make soft tortillas:

- Lay a stack of up to 12 tortillas in a clean, heavy kitchen towel and wrap securely.

- Put a pan large enough to hold the tortillas on the stove. Add 1/2 inch water.

- Place a metal vegetable steamer over the water and make sure it's not touching the water.

- Lay the wrapped stack of tortillas in the steamer. If preparing 24 tortillas, use a pan and metal rack large enough to hold the stacks side by side.

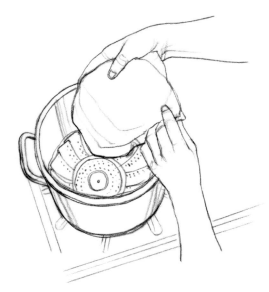

- Cover the pan and bring the water to a boil. Let it boil for 1 minute.

- Turn off the heat. Without opening the pan, let it sit for at least 15 to 20 minutes.

- Serve the tortillas warm.

- You can keep the tortillas warm by simply returning the pan with the wrapped tortillas to the heat and boiling for 1 minute every hour. Or you can place the covered steamer, after it has boiled, in a 200°F oven and keep the tortillas warm for up to 1 hour.

Serve!

- To make it easy for your guests, arrange the fillings, shredded lettuce, cheese, and tortillas all within easy reach.

- If you have a food-warming tray, this is a great time to use it to keep the meats, rice, and beans warm as your party goes on. If you don't have a warming tray, foods can be kept warm on the stove and served in covered dishes.

- Keep your eye on the serving table and refill your dishes as they run low. Most importantly, have fun!

Mexican Sauce *Salsa Pico de Gallo*

Did you know that salsa outsells ketchup as the most popular condiment in the United States? What makes salsa so popular is its fresh taste. It goes so well with just about everything. You may be tempted to make this popular sauce recipe in a blender, but don't—the end result will be more like salsa soup. Mexican Sauce is best made about one hour before you are ready to serve it, so its flavor can come to life.

Serves 6

ingredients

3 medium-size ripe tomatoes or 4 or 5 Roma tomatoes (about 1½ pounds)

1 to 3 fresh serrano or jalapeño peppers (or to taste)

1 small white onion

10 to 12 sprigs fresh cilantro

1 lime

1 teaspoon salt

On your mark . . .

• Wash the tomatoes and remove the stem circle at the top.

• Cut the tomatoes in half, then cut each half into 1/4-inch-thick slices.

• Cut the slices into small chunks and, using a spoon, scoop up the tomatoes into a medium-size bowl.

Get set . . .

• Slip on a pair of rubber or latex kitchen gloves.

• Slice the stem end off the peppers. Cut the peppers in half lengthwise. Rinse out the seeds and discard.

• Finely chop or mince the peppers and add to the tomatoes. Rinse the gloves and remove them.

• Peel and finely chop the onion, measure 1/2 cup, and add to the tomatoes.

• Wash the sprigs of cilantro, shake off the excess water, and chop them. Add to the bowl.

• Cut the lime in half and squeeze the juice into the tomato mixture. Add the salt.

• Mix the ingredients together, cover, and let the salsa rest for about 1 hour.

Serve!

• Place in your favorite bowl and serve together with tortilla chips and green salsa.

Green Salsa *Salsa Verde*

You have seen it on store shelves and on the tables at Mexican restaurants. Now you can make it at home and experience the real taste treat that is *salsa verde*. Use it to top Red Enchiladas (page 87) or Little Pork (page 82), or alongside a bowl of crispy Tortilla Chips (page 76). However you decide to use it, you will be making this recipe again and again.

Serves 6

ingredients

2 cloves garlic
½ small white onion
1 pound tomatillos
8 to 10 fresh cilantro sprigs

1 or 2 fresh jalapeño peppers (or to taste)
3 cups water
2 teaspoons salt
1 tablespoon corn or canola oil

On your mark, get set . . .

- Peel the garlic and leave whole.
- Peel the onion, chop into small pieces, and set aside.
- Peel off the papery outer husks from the tomatillos. Wash them with cold water.
- Wash the cilantro sprigs and shake to remove excess water. Pat dry and set aside.
- Remove the stems from the jalapeños.

Cook!

- Add the water, garlic cloves, tomatillos, whole jalapeños, and salt to a 3-quart pan.
- Bring to a boil on medium-high heat. Reduce the heat to low and simmer, uncovered, for 10 minutes.
- Drain mixture in a colander, reserving 1/2 cup of the cooking liquid.
- Ask your adult assistant to help with the next steps.
- Add the tomatillo mixture, cilantro, and reserved cooking liquid to the jar of a blender.
- Press the lid almost completely in place, leaving it slightly ajar. Blend at low speed for a few seconds. Now press the lid firmly in place and blend at high speed for about 10 to 15 seconds, or until liquefied.
- Remove the jar from the blender and place it near the stove.
- Heat the oil in a 10-inch frying pan on medium heat for 20 seconds.
- Add the chopped onion. Cook for 4 to 5 minutes, or until the onion begins to brown.
- Remove the pan from the heat and pour in the liquid from the blender. Have a lid close by, as the mixture will bubble and boil when it hits the hot pan. Cover the pan for a few seconds to prevent spattering.
- Remove the cover and cook on low heat for about 5 minutes, stirring occasionally.
- Let cool completely and serve.

Tortilla Chips *Tostadas*

Most of us are familiar with the tortilla chips sold in our local supermarket. In Mexico it is much more common to make these crispy chips fresh at home. Once you try your first batch of homemade Tortilla Chips, you might wonder why you've never made these delicious chips before. This recipe offers two ways to cook the chips—frying or baking. The baked ones are lower in fat and just as delicious. Whichever method you choose, be sure to have on hand lots of **Guacamole (page 78), Green Salsa (page 74)**, or **Mexican Sauce (page 73)** to scoop up and enjoy.

Makes 72 chips

ingredients

12 corn tortillas (See page 162)
¾ cup canola oil (for frying)
salt to taste (optional)

On your mark . . .

- On a cutting board, place 6 of the tortillas on top of each other like a stack of pancakes.

- Repeat with the remaining 6 tortillas, making 2 stacks.

- Cut each stack in half, then cut each half into 3 wedges.

Get set . . .

- Spread out all the wedges on a clean tray. Cover them loosely with a clean towel and let them dry for about 20 to 30 minutes.

Cook!

To fry the chips:

- You will need a large metal slotted spoon and paper towels. Have your adult assistant handle the frying.

- Place a 10- to 12-inch heavy-bottomed or cast-iron frying pan on the stove and add the oil. It should be about 1 inch deep in the frying pan; if not, add more oil.

- Heat the oil on medium to medium-high heat for 3 to 4 minutes, or until a deep-fry thermometer reads 380°F.

- Add a small handful of the tortilla wedges to the hot oil. Stir carefully with the slotted spoon to keep them moving and separate. The chips will turn light brown and crispy; this will take about 1 minute.

- Remove the chips with the metal slotted spoon and drain them on paper towels. If you are salting the chips, this is the time to sprinkle on the salt.

- Repeat until all the chips are fried and salted.

- Place the chips in a basket or bowl and serve.

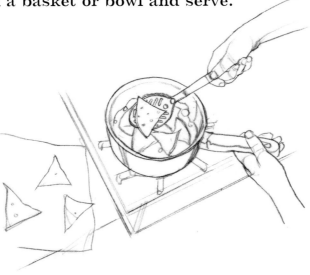

To bake the chips:

- You will need a baking tray and 2 wire cooling racks. Preheat the oven to 350°F.

- Place a cooling rack on the baking tray and spread some of the wedges over it in a single layer. Place the other rack upside down on the wedges to prevent them from curling.

- Bake the wedges for 12 to 15 minutes, or until crispy.

- Remove the tray from the oven. If you are salting the chips, this is the time to sprinkle on the salt.

- Repeat until all the chips are baked and salted.

- Place the chips in a basket or bowl and serve.

(See pages 68-69 for photo.)

Avocado Dip *Guacamole*

Guacamole is a recipe believed to have come from the ancient Aztec and Maya peoples. It's so popular today that it can be found on almost all Mexican restaurant menus. In Mexico this dip is commonly prepared in a *molcajete*, a bowl made from volcanic stone. Don't worry if you don't own one—a bowl and fork will work just as well. Follow this recipe exactly the first time, and then decide whether you want to use more or less of the pepper and salt to suit your taste. You can read about avocados in the Essential Ingredients section at the back of this book.

Serves 6

ingredients

½ small white onion
1 clove garlic
1 small fresh jalapeño
   or serrano pepper (or
   to taste)
1 medium-size ripe tomato
4 or 5 sprigs fresh cilantro

1 lime
3 ripe Hass avocados
1 teaspoon salt (or to taste)
crispy Tortilla Chips (page 76) to serve

On your mark . . .

- Peel and finely chop the onion and garlic and place them in a medium-size bowl.

- Slip on a pair of rubber or latex kitchen gloves.

- Slice the stem end off the pepper and cut the pepper in half lengthwise.
- Rinse out the seeds under cold running water and discard.

- Finely chop the pepper and add to the bowl. Rinse the gloves and remove them.

- Wash the tomato and remove the stem circle from the top. Chop the tomato into small chunks. Add them to the bowl, making sure to add any tomato liquid that may have escaped.

- Rinse the fresh cilantro, shake off the excess water, and pat dry with paper towels. Chop the cilantro and add to the bowl.

- Cut the lime in half and squeeze the juice into a small bowl. Measure 3 tablespoons and add to the tomato mixture.

- Toss together all the ingredients and set aside.

Get set . . .

- About 30 minutes before you are ready to serve the guacamole, prepare the avocados.

- To do this, lay an avocado on a cutting board. With the tip of a sharp knife, start at the stem end and cut all the way lengthwise around the avocado. Remember that there is a large pit inside, so don't try to cut through it.

- Now pick up the avocado and, holding it with both hands, twist each half in opposite directions to separate the halves. Scoop out the pit with a table-spoon, but don't throw it away.

- Scrape the pulp of the avocado away from the skin and add it to the bowl with the tomato mixture.

- Repeat with the remaining avocados. Add the salt.

- Gently mash the avocados with a wooden spoon or a fork, combining all the ingredients. Don't overmash the guacamole; it should be chunky.

- Put the pits in the bowl. This will keep the dip from changing color.

- Cover the guacamole with a sheet of plastic wrap pressed directly on the sur-face until ready to serve.

Serve!

- Remove the pits, if you like, and place the dip in a serving bowl.

- Surround the dip with crispy Tortilla Chips and serve immediately.

(See pages 68-69 for photo.)

Ground Meat Filling for Tortillas

Picadillo

Picadillo is one of Mexico's many culinary treasures. A warm tortilla stuffed with this sweet and lightly spiced filling is irresistible. *Picadillo* can be used in tacos, enchiladas, or as a stuffing for zucchini or other vegetables. This recipe can be made with a combination of ground pork and beef, or you can choose to use all beef or all pork.

Serves 4 to 6

ingredients

2 dried ancho chiles
½ cup hot water
1 medium-size white onion
2 large ripe tomatoes or
   1 cup canned chopped
   Italian plum tomatoes
2 cloves garlic
10 to 12 pimento-stuffed
   olives
1 teaspoon ground cinnamon

¼ teaspoon ground cloves
½ cup raisins
½ cup slivered almonds
½ teaspoon freshly ground black pepper
1 teaspoon salt
1 teaspoon brown sugar
2 tablespoons olive or vegetable oil
1 pound ground beef (sirloin or top round)
⅓ cup chicken stock or water

On your mark, get set . . .

- Place the ancho chiles in a bowl, cover with 1/2 cup hot water, and let stand for 15 minutes.

- Peel and coarsely chop the onion and measure 1 cup.

- If using fresh tomatoes, wash them and cut out the stem circle at the top. Chop the tomatoes into chunks and measure 1 cup.

- If using canned tomatoes, drain them and measure 1 cup.

- Crush, peel and chop the garlic. Chop the olives.

- Measure the cinnamon, cloves, raisins, almonds, black pepper, salt, and brown sugar and set aside.

Cook!

- Heat a 10- to 12-inch frying pan with the oil on medium-high heat for 30 seconds.

- Add the ground meat and sauté for 4 to 5 minutes, or until the meat is no longer pink, breaking it up with a spoon or spatula as it cooks.

- Using a slotted spoon, remove the meat to a bowl and keep close by.

- Remove the chiles from the soaking water and squeeze out the excess liquid, but do not discard it. Remove the stems and coarsely chop the chiles.

- Reheat the frying pan on medium-high heat for 30 seconds.

- Add the onion, chopped chiles, chile soaking liquid, garlic, and chopped olives. Cook for 3 to 4 minutes.

- Reduce the heat to medium. Add the tomatoes and chicken stock and cook for 5 minutes, stirring occasionally.

- Return the meat to the frying pan.

- Add the cinnamon, cloves, raisins, almonds, black pepper, salt, and brown sugar. Stir well to combine all the ingredients.

- Cover the pan, reduce the heat to low, and simmer for 8 to 10 minutes. Serve hot.

Little Pork *Carnitas*

These "Little Meats" are so popular all over Mexico that each region has its own version. This recipe is from Uruapan in the state of Michoacán in central Mexico. These delicate little chunks of pork are just the right thing to put inside tacos or Red Enchiladas (page 87), or to enjoy on their own as a great lunch or dinner. Spoon on some homemade Green Salsa (page 74) and you have something so tasty you may call them anything but "little."

Serves 6

ingredients

1 small white onion
2 cloves garlic
2 pounds boneless pork loin end, with a little fat
1½ teaspoons salt

1 teaspoon dried oregano
8 cups cold water
1 large fresh orange
½ cup whole milk
2 tablespoons canola oil

On your mark, get set . . .

- Peel the onion and cut into large chunks. Crush, peel, and chop the garlic.

- Cut the pork into 2-inch cubes, leaving a small amount of fat on each piece.

- Measure the salt and oregano and set aside.

Cook!

- Place the onion, garlic, pork cubes, water, salt, and oregano in a 6-quart heavy-bottomed pan with a lid.

- Cover the pan and bring the mixture to a boil on medium heat.

- Reduce the heat to medium-low and simmer for about 1 hour, or until the pork is tender but not falling apart.

- In the meantime, squeeze the orange and measure 3/4 cup juice. Measure the milk and set aside.

- When the pork is ready, drain the meat in a colander and discard the cooking broth.

- Reheat the pan on medium heat with 1 tablespoon of the oil for about 20 to 30 seconds.

- Add the orange juice and milk. Add the pork.

- Cook, uncovered, for 5 to 10 minutes. As the pork cooks, the liquid will begin to evaporate.

- Add the remaining 1 tablespoon oil and, using a spoon, mix it into the pork as it cooks. Cook for another 5 to 7 minutes. The pork will turn brown and crispy.

- Place a metal colander inside a heatproof bowl and have it ready next to the stove. When the meat is brown and cooked, remove it to the colander to drain.

- Serve hot as a filling for tacos or Red Enchiladas.

chef's tip

TO SAVE TIME, YOU CAN ASK THE BUTCHER TO CUT THE MEAT INTO 2-INCH CHUNKS. WHEN CHOOSING PORK FOR THIS DISH, IT IS IMPORTANT TO FIND A PORK LOIN END CUT, WHICH STILL HAS SOME FAT ON IT. THIS WILL HELP KEEP THE PORK MOIST AS IT COOKS. IF YOU CHOOSE A LEANER CUT, THE PORK MAY BE DRY. IF YOU CAN'T FIND A PORK LOIN END CUT, YOU CAN USE PORK SHOULDER.

Chicken Breasts in Stock
Pechugas de Pollo

This recipe is a quick way to prepare chicken breasts for tacos or enchiladas. You can substitute chicken thighs or try a combination of both. The broth that is left after cooking the chicken is excellent for using in soups or sauces, so be sure to save it.

Serves 4

ingredients

1 carrot
1 stalk celery
1 clove garlic
1 small bunch fresh parsley
2 chicken breasts with bone and
   skin, preferably organic/free-range
   (about 10 ounces)

4 cups water
½ small white onion
1 teaspoon salt
freshly ground black pepper
   to taste

On your mark, get set . . .

- Wash, but don't peel, the carrot and celery and coarsely chop.

- Crush and peel the garlic.

- Wash the parsley in cold water.

Cook!

- Put the chicken in a 4-quart stockpot with the rest of the ingredients and bring to a boil.

- Reduce the heat to low and simmer for 35 to 40 minutes, or until the chicken is tender and cooked through to the bone. Skim off any foam that rises to the surface during cooking.

- Drain the chicken in a strainer, reserving the stock. Discard the vegetables.

- Completely cool the stock and refrigerate it for another recipe. Chicken stock will keep for 1 week in the refrigerator or up to 3 months in the freezer.

- After the chicken has cooled, remove the skin and discard. Pull the meat from the bone.

- Shred the chicken into long strips. It is now ready for use in tacos or enchiladas.

(See pages 68-69 for photo.)

White Rice *Arroz Blanco*

This basic rice has so many different uses in Mexican cooking that you will want to make plenty of it to keep on hand as an authentic addition to your menu.

Serves 4 to 6

ingredients

1 cup long-grain white rice
1 cup hot water
1 medium-size white onion
1 clove garlic

2 tablespoons canola or olive oil
2 ½ cups homemade Chicken Stock, page 12, or canned low-sodium, or water
1 teaspoon salt

On your mark, get set . . .

• Place the rice in a large bowl and cover with the hot water. Let stand for 15 to 20 minutes.

• Pour the rice into a strainer, shake to remove the excess water, and let drain.

• Peel and chop the onion and garlic into small pieces and set aside.

Cook!

• Heat a heavy-bottomed frying pan with the oil on medium heat for 30 seconds.

• Give the rice one more shake and add it to the frying pan. Cook the rice for 4 to 5 minutes, or until all the grains are coated with oil and begin to color slightly.

• Add the onion and garlic. Cook for 8 to 10 minutes, stirring well to keep from sticking.

• Slowly add the broth or water and the salt and bring to a boil. Cook, uncovered, at a gentle boil for another 10 to 12 minutes, or until the liquid is absorbed and tiny air holes cover the surface of the rice.

• Remove the pan from the heat and cover tightly. Set in a warm place for at least 20 minutes.

• When ready to serve, stir the rice with a fork to loosen and separate the grains and serve hot.

(See pages 68-69 for photo.)

Red Enchiladas *Enchiladas Rojas*

What dish is more recognizably Mexican than enchiladas? This recipe is from Aguascalientes in the central region of Mexico. Making enchiladas can be messy. Wear an apron, take your time, and most importantly, read the recipe completely to make sure you have everything you need close by.

Serves 6

ingredients

Sauce
3 medium-size ripe tomatoes or
   2 cups canned whole tomatoes
2 dried ancho chiles
2 dried pasilla chiles
1 small white onion
1 clove garlic
1 cup hot water
1 tablespoon corn or olive oil
1½ cups homemade Chicken Stock,
   page 12, or canned low-sodium
1 teaspoon salt

Enchiladas
2 cups Chicken Breasts in Stock
   (page 84)
12 corn tortillas
1 cup grated Mexican
   queso fresco, feta, or Monterey
   Jack cheese

On your mark, get set . . .

- If using canned tomatoes, drain them, measure 2 cups, and set aside.

- Place a dry heavy-bottomed or cast-iron frying pan on medium heat. Lay the whole dried chiles and the whole unpeeled fresh tomatoes, onion, and garlic in the frying pan.

- Roast the chiles for 1 to 2 minutes on each side, turning with a pair of tongs.

- Remove the chiles and place them in a bowl. Cover with 1 cup hot water and let stand for 20 to 30 minutes.

- Cook the rest of the ingredients in the frying pan for another 4 to 5 minutes, turning them occasionally. Don't worry if the tomatoes, onion, and garlic acquire burned spots—that will add great flavor.

- Remove the vegetables from the pan and let cool.

- Remove the stems and seeds from the soaked chiles and discard. Reserve the soaking liquid.

- Cut out the stem circle from the cooled tomatoes and discard. Peel the cooled garlic and onion.

- Coarsely chop the tomatoes, onion, and garlic.

- Ask your adult assistant to help you with this next step. Place the tomatoes (fresh or canned) in the jar of a blender along with the onion, garlic, chiles, and the chile soaking liquid. Press the lid firmly in place and blend the sauce at high speed until it liquefies. Pour into a bowl.

- Heat 1 tablespoon of the oil in the frying pan on medium heat for 20 seconds.

- Add the sauce. It will bubble and boil, so have a lid close by to cover the pan for a few seconds to prevent spattering.

- Reduce the heat to low. Add the chicken stock and salt to the sauce and cook on low heat for 10 to 15 minutes. Reduce the heat to simmer.

Cook!

- Preheat the oven to 350°F.

- Measure 2 cups of the shredded chicken and set aside.

- Warm a tortilla in a dry skillet on low heat for 1 minute on each side, turning it with a pair of tongs. This will soften the tortilla and make it easier to roll. Still using the tongs, dip it into the sauce to completely coat it. Lay the tortilla on a clean plate.

- Place about 2 1/2 tablespoons of the shredded chicken and about 1 tablespoon of the cheese on the tortilla.

- Roll up the tortilla and place it in a 10-inch baking dish, seam side down. You just made an enchilada!

- Repeat these steps until all the tortillas are warmed and filled.

- Pour the remaining sauce over the top of the completed enchiladas. Sprinkle on the remaining cheese.

- Bake the enchiladas for 4 to 6 minutes, or until the cheese is melted.

- Serve with White Rice (page 85) and Refried Beans (page 90).

Beans Cooked in a Pot *Frijoles de la Olla*

There is nothing quite like the wonderful aroma from a pot of simmering beans. Beans are one of Mexico's essential and deliciously simple ingredients. This classic recipe has been used by Mexican cooks for many years. Traditionally beans were cooked in clay pots called *ollas*, which were buried in the hot coals of the daily cooking fire. You can always buy canned beans, but when you discover how easy it is to make homemade beans, you just might decide to leave the can opener in the kitchen drawer. This recipe includes directions for making Mexican Refried Beans. You may think that "refried" means the beans are cooked over and over. What it really means is "cooked well" or "thoroughly" until the liquid is gone.

Serves 6

ingredients

1 pound (2½ cups) pinto, black, navy, or pink beans
6 to 8 cups water
1 small white or yellow onion

1 clove garlic (optional)
2 tablespoons bacon drippings, vegetable oil, or lard
2 teaspoons salt

On your mark . . .

- Rinse the beans with cold water in a colander.

- Shake off the excess water and pour the beans onto a clean tray in a single layer. Carefully check for and remove any tiny stones or shriveled, very dark beans.

- Place the beans in a 4-quart pot and cover with enough water to come 1 inch over the top of the beans.

Get set . . .

- Peel and chop the onion into small chunks.

- Crush, peel, and chop the garlic.

Cook!

- Place the pot of beans on medium heat. Add the onion, garlic, and bacon drippings or other fat, and bring to a boil.

- Partially cover the beans, reduce the heat to low, and cook at a gentle simmer for 1 1/2 to 2 hours, or until very tender. Now and then check the level of water in the pot. Make sure it stays about 1 inch over the top of the beans. If you need to add water, add hot water only, to keep from stopping the cooking process.

- When the beans are tender and almost completely cooked, add the salt and cook, uncovered, for another 10 to 15 minutes.

- Turn off the heat and let the beans cool completely.

- When ready to serve, reheat the beans gently on medium-low heat, stirring occasionally, until bubbly hot. Serve in bowls.

Refried Beans *Frijoles Refritos*
Serves 6 to 8

ingredients

1 small white onion

4 cups cooked pinto, black, navy, or pink beans (canned or fresh), undrained

2 tablespoons vegetable or canola oil, bacon or sausage drippings, or lard

2 teaspoons salt (optional)

½ cup Monterey Jack, Feta, Parmesan, or crumbled Mexican queso fresco cheese

½ cup tortilla chips

On your mark, get set . . .

- Peel and chop the onion into small pieces.

Cook!

- Place the beans in a 2- to 4-quart pot on low heat and cook for 15 to 20 minutes, stirring occasionally.

- Heat the oil or other fat in a 10- to 12-inch heavy-bottomed frying pan on medium heat.

- Add the onion and sauté about 8 minutes, or until golden brown, being careful not to let it burn. If the onion browns too fast, reduce the heat to low.

- Remove the beans from the cooking liquid with a slotted spoon and add about one-third of them to the frying pan. Using a round potato masher or the back of a large spoon, carefully mash the beans into a coarse texture.

- Add more beans and repeat this step until all the beans are added and coarsely mashed.

- Add 1 cup liquid, either the bean cooking liquid or hot water. Combine the beans and liquid.

- Cook the beans slowly for about 5 to 10 minutes, or until the liquid has almost completely cooked away.

- Taste the beans and add salt if needed. You probably won't need to add any if you are using canned beans.

- Just before serving, check the beans and add more liquid if they are too dry.

- Place the refried beans on a serving platter or in individual bowls, top with the cheese, and garnish with the tortilla chips. Serve hot.

A dish of warm Refried Beans, topped with cheese and ready to eat

All about Chile Peppers

Christopher Columbus made a mistake. In searching for that
most desirable of spices, black pepper, he thought he had found it when he first tasted
chiles. Chiles were spicy and hot, so he referred to them as "chilli peppers." Even though
he was not completely correct, the name stuck and the rest, as they say, is history.

Chiles have been a part of the Mexican kitchen for thousands of years. They add flavor
and excitement to any recipe they season. Did you know that chiles are a fruit from a
group of plants called *capsicum* and that there are over one hundred varieties? These
colorful fruits range widely in type, size, shape, and heat. They're packed with vitamins
A and C. Hot or mild, chile peppers are really very cool once you get to know them.

Many people incorrectly believe that all chiles are hot, so they won't even give
them a try. As a result, these healthy fruits are very misunderstood. "That will taste
too hot!" How many times have you said that to yourself when you've seen a dish on a
menu that has chile peppers in it? But the fact is that some are quite mild tasting.

There are a few important things to know before you begin to cook with chiles. Any
experienced cook will tell you that some precautions are essential to make sure your
cooking experience is a pleasant one. If you follow these simple guidelines, you'll get
the best results and give your dishes an authentic Mexican flavor.

How to Handle Chiles
Wear rubber or disposable latex kitchen gloves as a precaution to keep your skin from
contacting the hot oils in the pepper, called capsaicin, which can stay on unprotected
skin for several hours. Remember, never touch your eyes, nose, or any other part of
your face or skin when working with hot peppers, to avoid passing on the capsaicin.
Rinse your gloves and dry them with paper towels before removing them, and then
give your hands a thorough washing with hot soapy water.

How to Prepare Chiles for Recipes
Rule # 1: Slip on your rubber or latex gloves before beginning.

Preparing Fresh Chiles: Rinse the chile in cold water, never hot. Break off the stem,
pull it away from the chile, and discard. To open the chile, lay it on a cutting board
and slice it lengthwise with the tip of a sharp knife. Once it is open, you will notice the
seeds and the lighter-colored veins inside. These contain most of the heat. If you are
like most people and don't want your dish to be too hot, remove the seeds under cold
running water. If you like your recipe spicy, leave all or some of them.

Preparing Dried Chiles (Method #1): If the dried chile is very dusty, rinse it in cold water
and pat dry with a paper towel. Place the dried chile in a small bowl and add 1 cup of hot
water. In 20 to 30 minutes, the chile skin will soften and puff up slightly, looking more
like it did when it was fresh. Remove the stem and seeds and follow the directions in your
recipe. Save the soaking water to use for an extra-flavorful liquid in your recipes.

Preparing Dried Chiles (Method #2): Heat a dry heavy-bottomed or cast-iron frying pan
on medium-low heat for 3 to 4 minutes. Place the chile in the pan and cover it with a
small metal lid to flatten it. Toast the chile for 1 to 2 minutes on each side, or until the
skin begins to soften and change color. Remove to a bowl and follow the directions
above to soak the chile.

Types of Fresh Hot Chiles

JALAPEÑO: The jalapeño is probably the most familiar of all Mexican peppers. This famous rich green hot pepper can be found in salsas and sauces, stuffed with cream cheese, on a plate of nachos, spicing up a jar of pepper jam, or topping tacos. The jalapeño, which generally measures about 2 1/2 inches long and 3/4 inch wide, originated in Mexico. Available fresh or canned, it ranges from hot to very hot. You should not handle a jalapeño without gloves. Remove the veins and seeds from the inside before using it in your recipe.

Serrano: The serrano pepper is very popular in Mexico. It is smaller in size than a jalapeño and has a bullet shape. It is packed with heat and flavor; use it with caution.

Types of Dried Chiles

ANCHO: The ancho is reddish brown in color when dried and changes to a brick red when soaked in water. It is four to five inches long and packed with smoky flavor. The ancho is probably the most common dried pepper used in the cooking of Mexico. When fresh, it is called poblano and is dark green in color. The ancho can be soaked and ground for many different recipes. The heat ranges from mild to medium-hot.

CHIPOTLE: A chipotle is a jalapeño pepper that is dried and smoked. You can buy chipotles canned and packed in vinegar or in a sweet red sauce called adobo. You can also buy them dried. The smoking process fills the chile with a great deep flavor.

PASILLA: The pasilla is wrinkled, long and narrow, and raisin brown in color. In fact, in Spanish its name means "little raisin." Pasilla chiles are mild to medium-hot. They are best used in recipes for sauces and with seafood.

Chile Wisdom

You ate a chile that was just too hot and now your mouth is on fire?
Drink a glass of milk or have some yogurt or another dairy product. Try eating a piece of bread or tortilla. Do not drink water, as it will only make your problem worse.

You forgot to wear gloves and now your hands are starting to burn?
Soak your hands in cold salted water. Or add a tablespoon of bleach to a large bowl of cold water and soak until the burning fades. If all else fails, rub a little toothpaste on your skin.

You don't know how many chiles to use?
If you don't like a lot of heat, start with fewer chiles than the recipe calls for. It is easy to add heat to a recipe, but very difficult to take it away. If you find the dish just too hot after you've made it, you can cool it down by adding more tomatoes, rice, or potatoes, or by topping the dish with more cheese and sour cream.

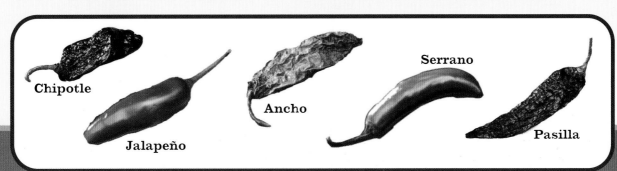

Chipotle

Ancho

Serrano

Jalapeño

Pasilla

vegetables and side dishes

Zucchini with Corn and Tomatoes

Calabacitas con Elote

This recipe comes from Oaxaca, at the southern coastal tip of Mexico. The Mexican cook would probably use fresh corn at the peak of the summer harvest, ripe tomatoes, and fresh-picked zucchini. If corn is not in season, this recipe works almost as well with frozen corn.

Serves 6

ingredients

1½ pounds fresh zucchini
2 medium-size ripe tomatoes
1 small white onion
1 clove garlic
2 sprigs fresh cilantro

2 ears fresh corn or 1 cup frozen corn
2 tablespoons canola oil
1 teaspoon salt
freshly ground black pepper to taste

On your mark, get set . . .

• Wash and scrub the zucchini very well with a vegetable brush to remove any dirt.

• Cut the zucchini in half lengthwise. Cut the halves lengthwise into 1-inch-thick slices. Cut the slices into cubes. Set aside.

• Remove the stem circle from the top of the tomatoes, chop the tomatoes into small chunks, and set aside. Peel and chop the onion and garlic.

• Wash the sprigs of cilantro to remove any sand and dry with paper towels. Chop and set aside.

• If using fresh corn, remove the kernels from the cob with a sharp knife. Ask your adult assistant to help with this step. If using frozen corn, measure the corn and set aside.

Cook!

• Heat the oil in a 12-inch frying pan on medium heat.

• Add the garlic and onion and cook for 2 to 3 minutes.

• Add the corn and zucchini and cook for 4 to 5 minutes.

• Add the tomatoes and raise the heat to medium-high. Bring the mixture to a fast boil.

• Add the cilantro, salt, and pepper and reduce the heat to low.

• Cover the pan and simmer for 5 to 7 minutes, or until the vegetables are tender but have not lost their color or crunch. Serve hot.

Vegetable Casserole *Ratatouille*

Ratatouille is the ultimate vegetable dish and it comes from Provence. Don't be discouraged that it takes a little extra time to prepare. The final results are worth the effort. Ratatouille is going to make you feel very differently about eating your vegetables!

Serves 6

ingredients

1 medium-size eggplant
3 medium-size zucchini
2 1/2 teaspoons salt
1 red onion
2 red bell peppers
1 clove garlic

3 medium-size ripe tomatoes (about 1½ to 2 pounds)
3 tablespoons chopped fresh flat-leaf parsley
5 tablespoons extra-virgin olive oil
freshly ground black pepper to taste

On your mark . . .

- Wash and peel the eggplant. Cut the eggplant into 1/2-inch slices, then cut each slice into quarters and measure about 3 cups.

- Wash the zucchini very well to remove any sand, then cut into 1/2-inch slices and measure about 4 cups.

- To remove excess moisture and bitter juices from the eggplant and zucchini, place them in two separate non-aluminum bowls and toss each with 1 teaspoon of the salt. Set aside for 20 to 30 minutes.

Get set . . .

- Peel and thinly slice the onion.

- Wash the peppers and cut in half. Remove the stems and seeds. Cut the halves into thin strips.

- Crush, peel, and chop the garlic.

- Wash the tomatoes and remove the stem ends. Chop the tomatoes into chunks and measure about 3 cups.

- Chop the parsley and set aside.

- Drain the eggplant and zucchini. To dry, lay a couple of sheets of paper towels on a tray or on the counter. Place the drained eggplant, a handful at a time, on the paper towels. Lay another sheet of paper towels over them and gently pat dry. Place the dried pieces in a bowl and repeat this step until all the eggplant and zucchini are dry.

Cook!

- Place a 2 1/2-quart heatproof casserole or heavy-bottomed pot, with a lid, next to the stove.

- Heat a 10- to 12-inch skillet with 1 tablespoon of the olive oil on medium heat.

- Sauté the zucchini slices for about 1 to 2 minutes on each side, until just beginning to brown. Remove them to a clean plate.

- Add 2 tablespoons of the olive oil to the skillet and sauté the eggplant, lightly browning on both sides, and place on a clean plate.

- Add the remaining 2 tablespoons olive oil to the skillet and sauté the onion and peppers for 10 minutes, or until they are soft.

- Add the tomatoes, garlic, remaining 1/2 teaspoon salt, and pepper. Cook for 5 to 7 minutes, or until the tomatoes start to release their liquid. Turn off the heat.

- Spoon about one-third of the tomato mixture into the bottom of the casserole. Top with one-third of the eggplant and one-third of the zucchini, then sprinkle on 1 tablespoon of the parsley.

- Make another layer with one-third more of the tomato mixture, one-third of the eggplant and zucchini, and 1 tablespoon of the parsley.

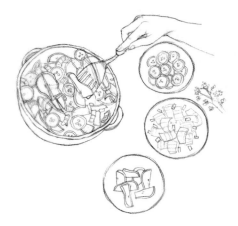

- Make the last layer with the remaining vegetables, following the same layering steps, and sprinkle with the remaining 1 tablespoon chopped parsley.

- Cover the casserole and place it on low heat. Bring the stew to a simmer and cook for 10 to 12 minutes. If it is cooking too fast, turn down the heat.

- Remove the lid and, using a hot pad, lift up one side of the casserole to allow any juices to flow to the opposite side. Baste the cooking vegetables with the juices. You may have to move some of the vegetables aside.

- Raise the heat slightly to medium-low. Cook uncovered for about 12 to 15 minutes. Baste the vegetables a few more times as they cook. The liquid will almost evaporate. When it does, turn off the heat and serve.

- Ratatouille can be served hot or cold and is delicious either way.

Glazed Carrots *Carottes Glacées*

The French have created many of the world's favorite vegetable dishes, and this recipe from Vichy, in central France, is just one example. Thanks to the versatility of French cooking, this ideal carrot recipe goes beautifully with chicken, fish, or pork and is also perfect just by itself. Once you prepare Glazed Carrots, with their touch of buttery sweetness, don't be surprised if they're asked for again and again.

Serves 6

ingredients

10 to 12 carrots (about 2 pounds)
bottled spring water or tap water
5 tablespoons butter

2 tablespoons sugar
1 teaspoon salt
2 to 4 tablespoons chopped fresh flat-leaf parsley

On your mark, get set . . .

- You will want to find carrots that are similar in size. Wash, trim, and peel the carrots, being careful not to remove too much of the carrot skin. Cut the carrots into quarters and then into 2-inch pieces. If the carrots are small and very fresh, leave them unpeeled and gently wash the skins to remove any dirt, then cut in half.

- Place the carrots in a 4-quart saucepan and add the water to just cover about 1/4 inch over the carrots.

Get set . . .

- Bring to a simmer on low heat and cook for about 4 to 5 minutes. Remove a carrot and taste it after it has cooled a bit. It should still be a little underdone.

- Add the butter, sugar, and salt to the saucepan.

- Raise the heat to medium-high and boil rapidly until the liquid has evaporated. This will take another 4 to 5 minutes. Don't leave the pan unattended or the carrots may burn. Shake the pan to help glaze the carrots.

- Add the chopped parsley and give the pan a final shake. Serve immediately.

(See pages 110-111 for photo.)

Green Beans with Tomatoes, Roman Style *Fagiolini alla Romana*

The people of Rome are surrounded by some of the most beautiful landscapes in Italy. The farmers grow outstanding vegetables, and the cooks of Rome know just what to do with them. Try this dish and you will know why vegetables are such an important part of Italian cooking. Enjoy it hot, or make it a day ahead and serve it cold as a salad.

Serves 6

ingredients

1½ pounds fresh green beans
1 cup canned chopped tomatoes
1 small onion
1 clove garlic

1 tablespoon extra virgin
  olive oil
1 tablespoon butter
2 teaspoons salt
2 or 3 sprigs fresh Italian
  parsley, chopped

On your mark, get set . . .

- Wash the green beans, snap in half, and drop into a bowl of cold water.

- Pour the tomatoes into a hand strainer to drain. Discard the tomato juice.

- Peel and chop the onion.

- Crush, peel, and chop the garlic.

Cook!

- Place a 10-inch skillet over medium-low heat and add the olive oil and butter.

- When the butter and oil start to bubble, add the onion and garlic. Cook slowly for 4 to 5 minutes, or until they are golden in color.

- Add the tomatoes and bring to a slight boil.

- Drain the green beans through a colander, then add them to the skillet, along with the salt. Carefully toss the beans with the tomatoes.

- Cover the pan, reduce the heat to simmer, and cook for 30 minutes, or until the beans are tender. Halfway through the cooking, raise the lid and check to see if the liquid has cooked away. If it has, add a few tablespoons of cold water.

- When ready to serve, add the chopped parsley and bring to the table in a serving bowl.

The Story of Rice

Rice is the most common grain in the world today. It feeds more people than any other grain and is cultivated in more than 110 countries. Rice is consumed every day, in one form or another, by half the world's population and has been for thousands of years.

The first rice fields were cultivated in the Yangtze River Valley in China more than eight thousand years ago. Chinese farmers still grow rice using ancient farming methods, because these methods do the best job of producing good rice.

Rice plays a big role in Chinese culture. It is part of the folklore of the nation. The Chinese believe it is bad luck to tip over a rice bowl. The biggest insult you can pay a person is to throw his or her rice bowl on the ground. Rice remains a sign of a prosperous and rewarding life. It is thrown at weddings as a symbol of good luck. In some regions of China, a wooden bowl of rice is offered as a remembrance on the altars of relatives who have died.

The Chinese generally like their rice plain because it often accompanies food that is hot and spicy. Rice goes well with meat, fish, and vegetables. Its flavor is plain and simple, and the other flavors in a dish blend together with it perfectly.

There are several types of rice from which you can choose. Short grain rice is the smallest. It tends to be sticky and starchy. Short grain rice is great for desserts like rice pudding. Medium grain rice is a little fatter and less starchy. Long grain and extra long grain rice are the most popular in China and are recommended for the recipes in this book.

You can also buy converted rice, which takes less time to cook because it is precooked. Apart from white rice, there is brown rice. Brown rice still has the outer coating that is polished away to yield white rice. While brown rice is highly nutritious, it is less popular in China than white rice.

After you open a bag of rice, it is best to store it in a canister or a glass jar with a tight-fitting lid. Keep it dry and it will stay fresh for a very long time.

Rice is the easiest food in the world to cook. You can steam it, boil it, or fry it. Electric rice cookers, which are becoming more popular in China—and in the United States as well—than ever before, do a great job of steaming rice.

Next time you see that tiny grain of rice, think about how many people it can feed and how many centuries it has been cultivated on earth. But most of all, think about how delicious it is going to taste with that wonderful stir-fry you are about to make.

Fried Rice *Chao Fan*

Fried rice is one of the most popular dishes in Chinese cooking. It is a great way to use leftover rice and turn it into a fast and delicious meal or the perfect side dish. The story goes that this dish was first created in the city of Yangzhou, in the eastern province of Jiangsu.

Serves 6

ingredients

3 cups cold cooked white rice
¼ pound fresh or frozen shrimp
  (if frozen, thaw before using)
3 extra-large eggs
1 cup diced roast pork or cooked ham
3 green onions
3 tablespoons canola or peanut oil

Sauce
1 tablespoon soy sauce
½ tablespoon oyster sauce
1 teaspoon sugar
1 teaspoon sesame oil
1 teaspoon minced fresh ginger
½ teaspoon salt

On your mark...

- Prepare the rice and chill it. If using leftover rice, separate any clumps with your fingers. This works best if your hands are wet. Measure 3 cups.

- Peel the shrimp and discard the shells. Cut the shrimp in half lengthwise. Rinse under cold running water, and pull out the vein and discard. Cut the shrimp into small pieces and refrigerate.

- Break the eggs into a bowl and lightly scramble with a fork.

- Dice the pork or ham by cutting it first into strips, then into 1/2-inch pieces. Measure 1 cup.

- Slice the green onions into 1/4-inch pieces.

- Measure 3 tablespoons canola oil and set aside.

- Combine the ingredients for the sauce with a spoon and set aside.

Get set...

- Line up these ingredients on your countertop: canola oil, eggs, shrimp, rice, sauce, roast pork or ham, green onions.

Cook!

- Heat a wok on medium-high heat for 30 seconds. Add the eggs and cook for 1 minute, breaking them up with a spatula into very small pieces. Remove the eggs to a small bowl.

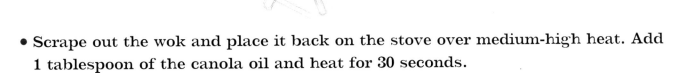

- Scrape out the wok and place it back on the stove over medium-high heat. Add 1 tablespoon of the canola oil and heat for 30 seconds.

- Add the shrimp and cook for 2 minutes. The shrimp should be bright pink when cooked. Remove the shrimp.

- Add the remaining 2 tablespoons of oil and reheat the wok for 30 seconds. Add the rice. Using the spatula, spread the rice around the wok to make sure all the grains get as much heat as possible. Cook for about 1 minute.

- Add the sauce and mix well, coating all the rice. Cook for 2 minutes, stirring constantly.

- Add the shrimp, eggs, roast pork or ham, and green onions. Combine all the ingredients, using the spatula. Cook for another minute or two, or until everything is hot. Serve hot.

White Rice *Bai Mi Fan*

The most basic part of any Chinese meal is the rice. There are many different types of rice you can buy. For the recipes in this book, long grain or extra long grain rice is recommended. You can follow the directions on the package, or try this authentic recipe.

Serves 6

ingredients

1 cup extra long grain white rice
1 3/4 cups water
1 teaspoon salt (optional)

On your mark...

• Pour the rice into a hand strainer.

• Rinse under cold running water a minute or two to remove the starch. Using a chopstick, a spoon, or your fingers, stir the rice as you rinse it. You will know the rice is ready to cook when the water running out of the strainer is clear.

Get set...

• Place the rice and salt in a 2-quart saucepan and add 1 3/4 cups water.

• Let the rice and water stand, uncovered, for at least 10 minutes or up to an hour. This will help to soften the rice.

Cook!

• Place the rice over high heat. Bring to a full boil. Continue to cook for 1 minute on high heat.

• Cover the pan, reduce the heat to the lowest setting, and cook for 20 minutes. Don't be tempted to lift the lid and peek at the cooking rice.

• After 20 minutes, turn off the heat and let the rice rest on the burner for 10 minutes.

• When ready to serve, stir with a chopstick or spoon to loosen the grains and fluff the rice.

(See page 104 for photo.)

Scalloped Potatoes *Gratin Dauphinois*

From the town of Grenoble in the French Alps comes this famous potato dish. There are many versions of Scalloped Potatoes, but there is only one Gratin Dauphinois. Try it served with Roast Chicken (page 112) or as a vegetable main dish.

Serves 6

ingredients

4 or 5 Idaho potatoes
    (about 2 pounds)
1 ½ cups whole milk
¼ cup heavy cream
2½ tablespoons butter

1½ teaspoons salt
¼ teaspoon freshly ground
    black pepper
¼ teaspoon freshly ground
    nutmeg
½ cup grated Swiss cheese

On your mark, get set, cook!

• Preheat the oven to 375°F.

• Wash, peel, and slice the potatoes in half lengthwise. Lay a potato half flat side down and cut into 1/4-inch slices. Repeat with the remaining potatoes. Measure 6 cups and set aside.

• Measure the milk and cream, combine them in a small saucepan, and place on low heat.

• Butter the sides and bottom of a 3- to 4-quart ovenproof baking dish with 1 tablespoon of the butter. Cut the remaining 1 1/2 tablespoons butter into small chunks and set aside.

• Lay the sliced potatoes in the baking dish in overlapping layers. Season the layers with the salt and pepper.

• When the milk and cream come to a boil, add the nutmeg and pour over the potatoes.

• Sprinkle on the grated cheese and dot with the remaining butter chunks.

• Wipe clean any splashes on the rim of the baking dish. Bake the gratin for 1 hour 10 minutes, or until the top is crusted and lightly golden brown. Serve hot.

main dishes

Roast Chicken *Poulet Rôti Entier*

The French are masters at many things in the kitchen, and roast chicken is unquestionably one of them. Baking a chicken to a golden brown with crispy skin is not difficult. The first thing to remember is that the freshest chicken makes the best roast chicken. If possible, look for organic, free-range chickens. Follow the steps to prepare the chicken carefully before it goes in the oven, along with a few simple food safety tips, and you're guaranteed a great-tasting chicken.

Serves 4

ingredients

1 whole chicken, preferably organic/free-range (3 1/2 to 4 pounds)
salt and freshly ground black pepper to taste
cotton string or butcher's cord
1 tablespoon butter or olive oil
1 carrot

1 stalk celery
1 onion
1 cup homemade Chicken Stock, page 12, or canned low-sodium chicken broth
1 tablespoon butter

On your mark, get set . . .

- Preheat the oven to 450°F.

- Remove all the packing material the chicken is wrapped in and discard it. Inside the chicken you will probably find a package of chicken parts. Remove and save the parts for chicken stock, or discard them. Trim any excess fat from the chicken and discard.

- Rinse the chicken under cold running water and pat dry with a paper towel, inside and out; a dry chicken will roast to perfect golden brown. Season the inside of the chicken with a little salt and pepper.

- With a 36-inch length of cotton string or butcher's cord, tie the end of one leg on top of the other so they are crossed over and together. Fold the wings under in a "laid-back" fashion by taking the tip of each wing and folding it under itself. Pull the string under the chicken and wrap the wings together by pulling the string across the top of the wings. Pull snugly to make a tight bundle and tie the ends together to keep the string secure.

- Place the chicken, breast side up, on a rack inside a lightly oiled roasting pan. The pan should be about 2 inches deep and just large enough to hold the chicken.

- Rub 1 tablespoon butter or oil all over the skin of the chicken and season with salt and pepper. Wash your hands and all work surfaces with hot soapy water.

- Wash and chop the carrot and celery. Peel the onion, chop in large pieces, and set aside.

Cook!

- Place the roasting pan with the chicken on the lower middle rack of the oven. Set the timer for 25 minutes and bake the chicken without peeking.

- When the timer rings, reduce the heat to 350°F. Open the oven door and, using a large spoon, baste the chicken with the juices from the bottom of the pan. Ask an adult for assistance in basting.

- Scatter the chopped vegetables around the pan, close the oven door, and continue to bake. Set the timer for 40 minutes and when it rings, baste again.

- Set the timer for another 40 minutes and baste a final time. Total cooking time is 1 hour 45 minutes, or until a meat thermometer inserted in the thigh reaches 180°F.

- Prick the skin of the lower thigh with a fork. The juices that run from it should be clear, with no trace of pink color. If pink, let the chicken cook for another 5 to 10 minutes.

- Remove the chicken from the oven to a warm platter and let it rest for 20 minutes.

- Ask your adult assistant to remove the string and carve the chicken as you prepare the sauce from the pan drippings. To do this, tip the roasting pan slightly and remove and discard all but 1 tablespoon of the fat. Leave the cooked vegetables in the pan for added flavor.

- Place the roasting pan on medium heat on the stove and add the chicken stock. Bring it to a boil. Carefully scrape up any stuck bits from the bottom of the pan with a large spoon. Watch that the sauce does not burn.

- Continue to boil as you add the remaining 1 tablespoon butter and the sauce reduces. Boil for 6 or 8 minutes as the sauce thickens, then reduce the heat and simmer for 3 to 4 minutes, or until slightly thickened.

- Place the carved chicken pieces on a serving platter and pass the sauce at the table.

(See pages 110-111 for photo)

chef's tip

USE ONLY CORD THAT IS MADE OF NATURAL FIBERS; OTHERWISE IT WILL MELT IN THE OVEN AND THE CHICKEN WILL HAVE TO BE DISCARDED.

Chicken, Hunters' Style
Pollo alla Cacciatora

Nearly every region of Italy has a version of this dish. Although the technique of slow-cooking meats in a flavorful sauce is found all over Italy, this recipe is inspired by the cooking of the Veneto. Serve this recipe on its own or over pasta or pan-fried polenta.

Serves 4

ingredients

3 ½ pounds chicken (preferably organic), cut into 8 pieces
½ cup all-purpose flour
3½ teaspoons salt
freshly ground pepper to taste
1 small yellow onion
1 carrot
1 clove garlic
4 ounces fresh mushrooms

½ cup canned chopped tomatoes
2½ tablespoons extra virgin olive oil
2 tablespoons butter
2 tablespoons balsamic vinegar
½ cup homemade **Chicken Broth**, page 12, or canned low-sodium
½ tablespoon dried oregano
3 tablespoons chopped fresh Italian parsley
¼ cup freshly grated Parmigiano-Reggiano cheese

On your mark . . .

- Wash the chicken pieces and remove as much of the fat and skin as you can.

- Dry the chicken very well with paper towels to prevent spattering when you brown it.

- In a small bowl, mix the flour with 2 teaspoons of the salt and pepper to taste.

- Roll a piece of the chicken in the flour mixture. Then shake off any excess flour and place the piece on a platter.

- Repeat until all the chicken is floured. Set aside. Wash the cutting board and knives that were used with the raw chicken.

Get Set . . .

- Peel and thinly slice the onion.

- Wash and chop the carrot.

- Crush, peel, and finely chop the garlic.

- If the mushrooms have a lot of dirt on them, carefully brush them clean with a paper towel. Then cut them into quarters.

- Drain the tomatoes in a hand strainer.

Cook!

- Place a 12-inch skillet over medium heat and add the olive oil and butter.

- After the butter has melted and the foam disappears, brown the chicken pieces, a few at a time, on both sides, starting with the largest pieces first. It will take about 10 to 15 minutes to brown all the chicken.

- As the pieces brown, place them on a clean platter. Do not return the browned chicken to the platter that held the raw pieces.

- After the browning is complete, have an adult assistant help you pour out all the fat in the skillet except 1 tablespoon.

- Reheat the skillet on medium heat. Add the onion and cook for 3 to 4 minutes.

- Add the balsamic vinegar, bring to a boil, and cook for about 30 seconds.

- Add the carrot, garlic, mushrooms, tomatoes, chicken broth, oregano, and the remaining 1 1/2 teaspoons salt. Stir well and cook for 1 minute.

- Return the chicken to the skillet, spooning some sauce over each piece, and bring to a soft boil.

- Cover the pan with a tight-fitting lid and reduce the heat to simmer. Cook for 40 to 50 minutes, or until the chicken is very tender.

- To serve, spoon the sauce over the chicken, sprinkle the chopped parsley and grated cheese over the top, and bring to the table.

Clockwise from the left: Fontina, Romano, Parmesan, Parmigiano-Reggiano, and Mozzarella cheese

Stir-Fried Orange Chicken
Qiang Chao Chen Pi Ji

Here is an adaptation of a classic Hunan recipe. This dish is usually cooked with red chile peppers, and that adds lots of heat. This version eliminates the hot peppers, but it still has great flavor. It also does not deep-fry the chicken, making it lighter in fat and calories.

Serves 6

ingredients

2 medium-size partially frozen,
  *boneless skinless chicken
  breasts (about 10 ounces)
3 tablespoons canola oil

Sauce
1 orange
1 tablespoon soy sauce
2 tablespoons hoisin sauce
1 tablespoon apple cider vinegar
½ teaspoon cornstarch
¼ teaspoon ground white pepper

Marinade
2 tablespoons soy sauce
2 tablespoons balsamic vinegar
1 tablespoon water
1 teaspoon sesame oil
1 teaspoon finely chopped
  fresh ginger
½ teaspoon cornstarch

On your mark...

- Wash the partially frozen chicken under cold running water and pat dry with paper towels.

- On a cutting board, slice the chicken into long strips and then cut into 1-inch cubes. Place the chicken cubes in a medium-size glass bowl. Wash the cutting board and knife in hot, soapy water.

- In a small bowl, mix together all the ingredients for the marinade. Pour over the chicken cubes and refrigerate.

> *Note: Partially freezing the chicken breasts makes them easier to cut; 20 to 30 minutes should be enough time in the freezer to firm them. Remember to set a timer so you don't forget them!

Get set. . .

- For the sauce: Wash the orange and dry it. Using a potato peeler, peel off 6 slices of the skin (be careful not to cut too deeply into the orange). Cut the orange in half and squeeze out 1/4 cup juice. Remove any seeds that fall into the juice.

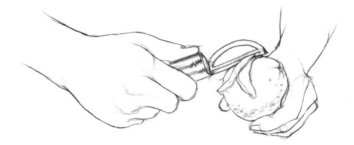

- In a small bowl, combine the juice, orange peels, soy sauce, hoisin sauce, cider vinegar, cornstarch, and white pepper. Mix well.

Cook!

- Place the sauce near the stove. Remove the marinated chicken from the refrigerator.

- Heat a wok on medium-high heat for 30 seconds. Add 1 tablespoon of the canola oil.

- After a few seconds, carefully add half the chicken cubes with about half the marinade. Spread the chicken in a single layer over the bottom of the wok and let it cook undisturbed for 2 minutes. Then give the chicken a good stir and let it cook for another 2 to 3 minutes, or until it is browned and a little crispy. Remove the chicken to a clean medium-size bowl.

- Reheat the wok for a few seconds and add another 1 tablespoon oil. Cook the rest of the chicken and marinade in the same way, removing when done.

Reheat the wok and add the remaining 1 tablespoon oil. Using a pair of tongs, lift the orange peels out of the sauce, add them to the hot oil, and stir-fry for a few seconds.

- Give the sauce a stir and pour it into the wok.

- Add all the cooked chicken. Stir-fry for another minute or so, or until the sauce thickens.

- Serve hot over rice.

Beggar's Chicken *Qi Gai Ji*

The legend goes that a very long time ago, this dish was created by a beggar who had stolen a chicken from a farmer. The beggar built a fire and put the chicken on a stick to roast it. Suddenly he heard the thunder of horses' hooves. The farmer! He quickly pulled the chicken off the fire, wrapped it in a lotus leaf, and buried it in the mud next to the fire. When the farmer came, he searched for his missing chicken but could not find it anywhere, so he galloped away. After he was gone, the beggar dug up the chicken. What a discovery! The mud around the lotus leaf had baked to a hardened clay. When the beggar cracked it open, he found a perfectly cooked, flavorful, and very moist chicken inside. He was very happy with his creation and ate the entire thing. This recipe for Beggar's Chicken comes from the western region of China.

Serves 6

ingredients

4 cups self-rising flour
1 ½ cups milk
3 tablespoons canola oil
extra flour for kneading
6 medium-size boneless skinless
chicken breasts
   (preferably organic)

½ pound ground pork
1 green onion, chopped
1 stalk celery, chopped
¼ cup chopped bamboo shoots
1 teaspoon salt
1 tablespoon hoisin sauce

On your mark...

• Place the flour in a large bowl. Combine the milk and 1 tablespoon of the canola oil, pour into the flour, and mix well into a soft dough.

• Turn the dough out onto a floured surface and knead until it is smooth. This will take a minute or two.

• Wrap the dough in plastic wrap or wax paper, place in a clean bowl, and cover with a kitchen towel. Let the dough rest at room temperature for about 30 to 40 minutes.

• Wash the chicken under cold running water and pat dry with paper towels. Place the chicken on a platter, cover, and refrigerate until ready to use. Wash the work area where the chicken was cleaned. Be sure to use lots of hot, soapy water and wipe the surfaces dry.

Get set...

- Heat a wok on medium-high heat for 30 seconds. Add 1 tablespoon of the canola oil and heat for a few more seconds.

- Add the ground pork and cook for 4 to 6 minutes, or until the meat browns slightly. Using a spatula, remove the pork to a clean bowl.

- Reheat the wok and add the remaining 1 tablespoon oil. Add the green onion, celery, and bamboo shoots, and stir-fry for 2 minutes.

- Return the pork to the pan and add the salt and hoisin sauce. Cook for another minute or two, making sure all the ingredients are well combined. This is the stuffing. You will need to let it cool completely in a bowl, cover, and refrigerate until ready to use.

Cook!

- Preheat the oven to 375°F.

- Unwrap the dough and cut it into 3 pieces. Then cut each of the pieces in half. Take 1 piece of dough and cover the rest with a clean cloth.

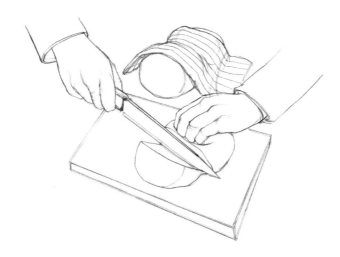

- Lightly flour the work surface. Using a rolling pin, roll out the dough to make a circle about 6 inches wide and 1/8-inch thick.

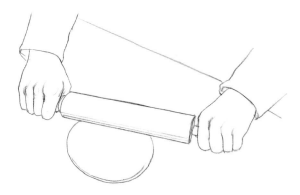

- Lay 1 chicken breast in the center of the dough and top with 1 1/2 tablespoons of the stuffing. Gently fold the dough up over the chicken and stuffing and press together at the edges to seal. Place the chicken in a well-greased baking pan.

- Repeat these steps with all the dough and chicken breasts.
- Bake for 45 to 50 minutes, basting the chicken with the juices in the bottom of the pan once or twice during the baking.
- Use a spatula to lift the chicken out of the baking pan when it is done.
- Serve hot.

Chicken in Almond Sauce
Pollo en Salsa de Almendras

Chicken in Almond Sauce comes from Oaxaca in the southern region of Mexico, a very exciting place to visit not only for its fascinating beauty but also to sample the local cooking.

Serves 6

ingredients

3½ pounds chicken, preferably organic/free-range, cut into 8 pieces

2 teaspoons salt

¼ teaspoon freshly ground black pepper

1 dried pasilla or ancho chile

½ cup hot water

1 small white onion

1 clove garlic

2 medium-size ripe tomatoes or 1 cup canned chopped tomatoes

1 lime

½ cup vegetable or canola oil

1 teaspoon ground cinnamon or one 2-inch piece stick cinnamon

3 whole black peppercorns

3 whole allspice

1 cup roasted whole almonds

2 cups homemade Chicken Stock, page 12, or canned low-sodium

On your mark . . .

• Rinse the chicken pieces in cold water. Pat dry and place in a large bowl.

• Sprinkle with 1 teaspoon of the salt and the black pepper and refrigerate.

• Break the stem top off the chile and discard. Tear the chile into small pieces and place in a bowl. Add the hot water and set aside to soften.

Get set . . .

• Peel and cut the onion into slices. Peel the garlic and leave whole.

• If using fresh tomatoes, wash and cut them into quarters.

• If using canned tomatoes, drain them and measure 1 cup.

• Squeeze the juice from the lime into a small bowl.

• Drain the chile and reserve the soaking liquid.

Cook!

• Heat a 4- to 6-quart heavy-bottomed pan with the oil on low heat.

- Add the onion, garlic, cinnamon, peppercorns, allspice, almonds, and chile. Cook for 8 to 10 minutes, stirring occasionally.

- Ask your adult assistant to help with the next steps.

- Lift the cooked ingredients out of the frying pan with a slotted spoon and place in the jar of a blender along with the tomatoes and the chile soaking liquid.

- Press the lid of the blender almost completely in place, leaving it slightly ajar. Blend at low speed for a few seconds. Now press the lid firmly in place, and blend at high speed for about 30 seconds.

- Pour the blended ingredients into a bowl and add the chicken stock.

- Add the remaining 1 teaspoon salt and stir to combine, then set aside.

- Reheat the pan on medium heat. Add the chicken, a few pieces at a time, and brown on all sides. Remove the browned chicken to a clean platter.

- Ask your adult assistant to drain off all but 1 tablespoon of the oil in the pan. Return the pan to the stove and place on medium heat.

- Pour in the blended ingredients. Have a lid close by to cover the pan for a few seconds to prevent spattering.

- Cook, uncovered, for 10 minutes, stirring occasionally. Add the chicken pieces and lime juice. Spoon the sauce over the chicken.

- Cover the pan and cook on low heat for 35 to 40 minutes, or until the chicken is cooked through to the bone. Serve hot with the sauce.

Country-Style Pork
Spezzatino di Maiale

In the south of Italy, between the sole and heel of the Italian boot, is a sun-bathed, ancient region called Basilicata. Here is an adaptation of a classic recipe from the town of Matera. The pork is baked in the oven in a heavy pot. Italian chefs like to use an enameled or cast-iron pot, but any heavy pot will work.

Serves 4

ingredients

2 ½ pounds center cut boneless pork loin

2 medium-size russet or Yukon gold potatoes

1 medium-size onion

3 cloves garlic

½ cup chopped fresh or canned tomatoes

½ teaspoon dried oregano or ½ tablespoon fresh

1 teaspoon dried rosemary or ½ tablespoon fresh

5 or 6 fresh basil leaves, torn into small pieces, or 1 teaspoon dried basil

2 teaspoons salt

¼ teaspoon crushed red pepper (optional)

¼ cup extra virgin olive oil

fresh Italian parsley for garnish

On your mark, get set . . .

- Preheat the oven to 375°F.

- Cut the pork loin into 1- to 1 1/2-inch cubes. Try to keep the cubes all about the same size so that they will cook evenly.

- Place the pork cubes in a heavy ovenproof pot and set aside. Wash the cutting board that you used for the pork.

- Rinse and scrub the potatoes, making sure to remove all the dirt.

- Leaving the skins on, cut the potatoes in half lengthwise. Cut each half into long slices, then cut the slices into 1-inch cubes. Add the potatoes to the pork.

- Peel and chop the onion, measure 3/4 cup, and add to the pork.

- Peel and chop the garlic and add to the pork.

- Next add the chopped tomatoes, oregano, rosemary, basil, salt, and crushed red pepper.

- Pour the olive oil over all the ingredients and carefully toss everything together with a large spoon.

Cook!

- Cover the pot and place on the middle rack of the oven.

- Bake for 1 hour. About halfway through the baking, use hot pads to carefully lift the lid, and stir the pot with a large spoon. Try to coat all the ingredients with sauce.

- After another 30 minutes, check to see if the pork and potatoes are tender. If they are, the dish is ready to serve. If the pork is not yet tender, bake for another 10 to 15 minutes.

- Spoon some of the sauce over the top, garnish with parsley, and serve hot.

Roast Pork with Dried Plums

Longe de Porc aux Pruneaux

This recipe comes from the heartland of France, the Loire Valley region. The richness of roasted pork and the subtle sweetness of the dried fruits make it perfect for a special occasion or holiday dinner. Why wait till then? Try it now and see how it will make any dinner a special occasion.

Serves 6

ingredients

½ cup dried pitted plums
½ cup dark raisins
1 teaspoon sugar
1 cup hot water
1 small onion
1 carrot
2 tablespoons butter
1 boneless pork loin roast
  (2½ pounds)

1 tablespoon balsamic vinegar
½ teaspoon dried thyme
½ teaspoon salt
¼ teaspoon freshly ground
  black pepper
½ cup homemade Chicken Stock,
  page 12, or canned low-sodium
  chicken broth
3 tablespoons heavy cream

On your mark, get set . . .

- Check the dried plums for pits and place the pitted plums in a small bowl.

- Add the raisins, sprinkle on the sugar, and add the hot water. Let the dried fruits soak for at least 30 minutes.

- Peel and chop the onion and measure 1/2 cup.

- Wash and chop the carrot and measure 1/2 cup.

Cook!

- Preheat the oven to 375°F.

- In a roasting pan large enough to hold all the ingredients, melt the butter on medium-low heat.

- When the butter begins to bubble, add the roast and turn it to brown on all sides. A sturdy pair of tongs works great for this. After the roast has browned, remove it to a clean plate.

- Add the onion, carrot, and balsamic vinegar to the roasting pan and cook for 2 to 3 minutes.

- Return the roast to the pan on top of the vegetables. Add the dried fruit mixture with the soaking liquid, thyme, salt, and pepper.

- Place the roasting pan on the middle rack of the oven and roast the pork uncovered for 1 1/2 hours. Every 1/2 hour, baste the roast with the liquid in the bottom of the pan.

- After 1 1/2 hours, the roast should be very tender and a meat thermometer placed in the center of the roast should read 165°F to 170°F. Remove the pork to a warm serving platter and loosely cover with foil.

- Place the roasting pan on the stovetop on medium-low heat and add the chicken stock. Bring to a simmer and cook for 2 to 4 minutes, skimming off and discarding any fat on the surface.

- Add the cream and cook for 2 to 3 minutes, but do not boil.

- Slice the roast into serving pieces and place on the platter, surrounded with the vegetables and fruit.

- Pour the finished sauce from the roasting pan into a separate serving bowl and pass it at the table.

Ginger Beef with Green Beans

Cong Jiang Niu Rou

Try this recipe from the provinces of Hunan and Szechwan. After you taste it, you will see why some Chinese call Hunan and Szechwan cooking the most distinctive in China. This recipe calls for a red chile pepper. If you decide to use it, be sure to read more about handling that hot little devil in the Essential Ingredients section at the back of the book.

Serves 6

ingredients

10 ounces fresh green beans
1 clove garlic
1 tablespoon balsamic vinegar
½ pound beef tenderloin
4 tablespoons peanut oil
½ cup dry-roasted peanuts
1 teaspoon salt
2 tablespoons soy sauce

Marinade
1 tablespoon balsamic vinegar
2½ teaspoons cornstarch
1½ teaspoons finely chopped
   fresh ginger
1 teaspoon sugar
1 green onion, cut into ¼-inch
   pieces

On your mark . . .

- Wash the green beans and string them: Start at the pointed end of the bean, pull the string down, and remove it. Cut the beans into 2-inch sections.

- Crush, peel, and finely chop the garlic.

- Mix 1 tablespoon balsamic vinegar with the garlic and pour over the beans. Set aside.

- Cut the beef tenderloin into thin slices. Stack the slices on top of each other a few at a time and cut them into strips. Place them in a glass bowl. Wash the knife and cutting board with hot, soapy water.

- In a small bowl, mix together the ingredients for the marinade. Pour over the beef strips and mix well. Refrigerate until ready to use, about 20 minutes.

Get set . . .

- Line up these ingredients on your countertop: peanut oil, green beans, peanuts, salt, marinated beef, and soy sauce.

Cook!

- Heat a wok on medium-high heat for 30 seconds. Add 2 tablespoons of the peanut oil.

- After 15 seconds, add the green beans, peanuts, and salt. Stir-fry for 3 to 4 minutes. The skin of the beans will darken and wrinkle. Remove the beans to a warm plate.

- Reheat the wok and add the remaining 2 tablespoons oil. Heat for 30 seconds.

- Add the marinated beef, a little at a time, until all the beef and marinade are added. Stir-fry for 3 to 4 minutes, using a spatula to move the beef around.

- Return the green beans to the wok. Add the soy sauce and stir-fry for another minute.

- Serve hot with rice.

Beef Stew with Tomatoes and Olives
Daube de Boeuf à la Provençale

Before ovens were common in French kitchens, cooking was done over open fires. Iron pots with lids hollowed out to hold hot coals slowly cooked many meals with wonderfully flavorful results. Slow-cooking, or braising, beef in a broth enhanced with vegetables creates the French stews that are some of the best in the world. Every region of France has its own version of this dish, but this recipe is an adaptation of a classic from Provence.

Serves 6

ingredients

For the beef

1 medium-size onion
1 clove garlic
2 carrots
3 medium-size ripe tomatoes
  (about 1 pound)
2 tablespoons red wine vinegar
1 cup Niçoise or pitted black olives

For the pot

½ pound thick-cut smoked bacon
3 tablespoons all-purpose flour

¾ cup homemade Chicken Stock,
  page 12, or canned low-sodium
  chicken broth
2 to 3 tablespoons chopped fresh
  flat-leaf parsley for garnish
½ pound mushrooms
2½ pounds top round or sirloin
  beef, cut into 1½-inch cubes
1 teaspoon salt
¼ teaspoon dried thyme

On your mark, get set . . .

- To prepare the beef: Peel and chop the onion into medium-size chunks and measure 1 cup.

- Crush, peel, and chop the garlic.

- Wash and chop the carrots and measure 1 cup.

- Wash the tomatoes and remove the stem ends. Cut the tomatoes into small chunks and measure 2 1/2 to 3 cups.

- Measure the vinegar and 1 cup drained pitted olives.

- Clean the mushrooms with a dry paper towel and cut into quarters.

- Place all the ingredients for the beef in a non-aluminum bowl large enough to hold everything, and mix well. Set the beef and vegetables aside to marinate.

- Cut the bacon into 3-inch pieces.
- Measure the flour and chicken stock and set aside.

Cook!

- Bring 1 cup water to a boil in a small saucepan on medium-high heat. Add the bacon pieces, reduce the heat to low, and simmer for 3 to 4 minutes. Drain the bacon and set aside.
- Place an ovenproof pot, with a lid, large enough to hold all the ingredients on the stove. Lay one-third of the bacon pieces on the bottom of the pot.
- With a slotted spoon, add about one-third of the marinated beef and vegetables on top of the bacon.

- Sprinkle on 1 tablespoon of the flour.
- Layer on another third of the bacon, then another third of the beef and vegetables, and top with 1 tablespoon flour.
- Make the last layer with the remaining bacon, then the beef, and top with the remaining 1 tablespoon flour.

- Pour any liquid left from the marinade over the top and add the chicken stock.

- Turn the heat to medium and bring the pot to a simmer. This will take about 10 minutes.

- Reduce the heat to low, cover the pan with the lid slightly ajar, and cook for 30 minutes, keeping the pot cooking at a gentle boil. If it is cooking too fast, reduce the heat.

- Preheat the oven to 350°F.

- After 30 minutes, remove the lid, cover the pot with a sheet of aluminum foil, and then replace the lid. Place the pot on the middle rack of the oven and bake for 1 hour 30 minutes.

- Serve hot, sprinkled with the chopped parsley.

chef's tip

THIS DISH CAN BE SERVED OVER BUTTERED EGG NOODLES, PREPARED ACCORDING TO THE PACKAGE DIRECTIONS. IF USING NIÇOISE OLIVES, REMOVE THE PITS BY GENTLY CRUSHING THE OLIVES WITH THE FLAT SIDE OF A LARGE KNIFE. DISCARD THE PITS.

Stir-Fried Shrimp and Red Peppers
Qing Jiao Xia

The southeastern region of China, including Kwangtung and its capital of Canton, has produced the most varied and popular cuisine in the country. The Cantonese are some of the most versatile cooks in all of China, and for good reason. Seafood comes from their coastal waters and fresh fish from their rivers. Their farms produce everything from prized vegetables to tropical fruits and nuts. Stir-Fried Shrimp and Red Peppers will introduce you to the popular combination of Chinese parsley, ginger, and garlic, blended with the flavor of fresh shrimp.

Serves 6

ingredients

1 pound medium-size shrimp
1 red bell pepper
1 green onion
3 tablespoons peanut oil
Chinese parsley (cilantro),
   2 tablespoons finely chopped

Marinade
2 tablespoons cornstarch
1 tablespoon soy sauce
1 tablespoon balsamic vinegar
1 teaspoon salt
1 egg white
1 clove garlic, crushed, peeled
   and chopped
2 slices fresh ginger (¼ inch
   thick), peeled and minced

On your mark...

• In a small bowl, combine the ingredients for the marinade and mix well.

• Peel the shrimp and discard the shells. Take 1 shrimp and lay it flat on a cutting board. Using a paring knife, make a slight cut in the outside curve of the shrimp. You will find a black vein. Remove it by pulling it out while rinsing the shrimp under cold running water. Repeat with the rest of the shrimp.

• Place the shrimp and marinade in a medium-size glass bowl, mix well, and refrigerate for 10 to 15 minutes.

• Wash the Chinese parsley, dry it with a paper towel, and chop it into small pieces. Measure 2 tablespoons.

Get set ...

• Wash the red pepper and cut in half. Remove the stem and seeds and discard. Cut the pepper into slices and then into 1/2-inch pieces.

- Slice the green onion into 1/4-inch pieces.
- Line up these ingredients on your countertop: peanut oil, shrimp, red pepper, green onion, Chinese parsley.

Cook!

- Heat a wok on medium heat for 15 seconds. Add 2 tablespoons of the peanut oil.
- After 30 seconds, add the shrimp a few at a time. Stir-fry for 2 to 3 minutes, or just until the shrimp turn pink. Remove the shrimp to a warm plate.
- Add the remaining 1 tablespoon oil to the wok. After 30 seconds, add the red pepper and stir-fry for 1 minute.
- Add the green onion, Chinese parsley, and shrimp. Stir-fry for about 1 minute, or until all the ingredients are well combined.
- Serve hot with rice.

Red Snapper from Veracruz
Pescado a la Veracruzana

Along the beautiful coastal waters of the Gulf of Mexico is the spectacular city of Veracruz. The Gulf of Mexico has an amazing assortment of seafood. Red snapper is so popular that it frequently gets star billing in local restaurants. This dish is a great example of how the cooking of Spain and Mexico combine to create an international hit that will have you taking the bows.

Serves 4

ingredients

1 small white onion
2 cloves garlic
2 to 4 canned or fresh
   jalapeño peppers
4 or 5 sprigs fresh cilantro
½ cup pimento-stuffed olives
½ teaspoon sugar
½ teaspoon ground cinnamon
¼ teaspoon ground cloves
1 teaspoon salt

1 teaspoon dried oregano
1 lime
2 large ripe tomatoes or 2 cups
   canned whole plum tomatoes
4 boneless red snapper fillets,
   about 8 ounces each
¼ cup extra virgin olive oil
1 tablespoon butter

On your mark . . .

- Peel and chop the onion into small pieces. Crush, peel, and chop the garlic.

- Slip on a pair of rubber or latex kitchen gloves.

- Cut the jalapeños in half, remove the stems and seeds, and chop into small chunks.

- Measure 2 tablespoons and set aside. Rinse the gloves and remove them.

- Rinse the cilantro sprigs and pat dry with paper towels. Chop the cilantro.

- Chop the olives and measure 1/2 cup.

- Measure the sugar, cinnamon, cloves, salt, and oregano and set aside.

- Squeeze the juice from half of the lime into a small bowl and measure
  1 1/2 tablespoons.

Get set . . .

- If using fresh tomatoes, wash them and remove the stem circle. Cut the tomatoes into quarters.

- If using canned tomatoes, drain them and measure 2 cups.

- Ask your adult assistant to help with this next step. Place the tomatoes in the jar of a blender and press the lid firmly in place. Blend the tomatoes at high speed for 20 seconds to liquefy. Pour into a bowl and set aside.

- Wash the fish fillets and pat dry with paper towels. Lay them in a lightly oiled oven-safe baking dish and keep refrigerated until ready to bake.

Cook!

- Preheat the oven to 425°F.

- Place the olive oil in a 3-quart pan on medium-low heat.

- Add the onion, garlic, and jalapeños, and cook for 6 to 8 minutes, or until the onion is very soft.

- Raise the heat to medium. Add the blended tomatoes, cilantro, olives, sugar, cinnamon, cloves, salt, oregano, and lime juice.

- Bring to a boil, then reduce the heat to low. Cook, uncovered, for about 12 minutes.

- Add the butter. Mix well. Remove from the heat and let cool for about 5 to 10 minutes.

- Spread the sauce evenly over the top of the fish fillets and bake for 20 to 25 minutes, basting once.

- Serve hot with rice.

desserts

Cream Puffs with Ice Cream and Chocolate Sauce *Profiteroles*

Cream puffs are magic. Just wait until you combine the next two recipes to create this famous dessert. Cream puffs filled with French vanilla ice cream and topped with Chocolate Sauce are what the French call profiteroles, but you will call them perfection! First make the cream puff dough and then the Chocolate Sauce. This is a dessert that will receive a standing ovation.

Makes 12 cream puffs

ingredients

1 stick unsalted butter
 (8 tablespoons) plus
 1½ teaspoons
1 cup all-purpose flour plus
 a little extra for dusting
½ teaspoon salt

1 cup water
4 large eggs (not extra-large
 or jumbo)
1 quart French vanilla ice cream
 or 1 recipe Whipped Cream
 (page 145)
1 recipe Chocolate Sauce
 (page 144)

On your mark, get set . . .

- Preheat the oven to 400°F.

- Lightly butter a large baking sheet with 1 1/2 teaspoons of the butter and dust with a tablespoon or so of the flour. Shake the baking sheet back and forth until the entire surface is coated with flour. Avoid touching the coated surface. Turn the sheet over and tap out the excess flour. Set the baking sheet aside.

- Measure 1 cup flour and 1/2 teaspoon salt and set aside.

Cook!

- Add the water, 1 stick butter, and salt to a medium-size saucepan, and place on low heat. Bring to a soft boil and cook until the butter has melted.

- Remove the pan from the heat, add the flour all at once, and stir very well with a wooden spoon for about a minute to make sure all the flour is mixed in.

- Place the pan back on the stove and turn the heat to medium. Continue to cook and stir for another 2 minutes. You will see a light film form on the bottom of the pan as you stir. Remove the pan from the heat.

- Pour the dough into a large bowl. Let it cool for about a minute.

- Add 1 egg and beat it into the mixture with an electric hand mixer on low speed. When it is completely mixed in, add another egg and mix in.

- Continue with the third egg and then the fourth. The last egg that is added should bring the dough together into a shiny yellow dough.

- To make the cream puffs: Use two tablespoons, one to scoop the dough and one to push the dough off onto the baking sheet in 12 rounded spoonfuls. Space the spoonfuls of dough about 3 inches apart. Give the tops a little tap to help round them.

- Bake for 40 minutes, or until puffed and golden. Remove the sheet from the oven and, with the tip of a sharp knife, pierce the cream puffs. This will allow the air to escape and dry the insides.

- Return the cream puffs to the oven and bake for another 10 minutes. Let cool completely.

- To serve: Cut each cream puff in half and place the bottom halves on 12 individual serving plates.

- Place 1 scoop French vanilla ice cream or Whipped Cream in the center of each half. Top with the other half of the cream puff.

- Spoon 1 tablespoon warm Chocolate Sauce over the filled cream puffs. Serve immediately.

(See pages 140-141 for photo.)

Chocolate Sauce *Sauce au Chocolat*

Can one ever say enough about the joys of chocolate? The French have found many delicious ways to use this dark, rich sauce, but none better than as the finishing touch on Cream Puffs (page 142). Chocolate Sauce will keep for up to a week in the refrigerator, but who ever heard of it lasting that long?

Serves 6

ingredients

½ cup water
3 tablespoons sugar
6 ounces semisweet chocolate

2 tablespoons unsalted butter
¼ cup cold whole milk
1 teaspoon vanilla extract

On your mark, get set, cook!

● Put the water and sugar in a heavy-bottomed 2-quart saucepan and bring to a boil on medium heat. Stir frequently to dissolve the sugar.

● Turn off the heat. Add the chocolate and butter and continue to stir until the sauce is smooth.

● Add the milk and vanilla and combine until the sauce is all the same color.

● Serve warm over Cream Puffs or ice cream.

(See pages 140-141 for photos of Chocolate Sauce and Whipped Cream.)

Whipped Cream *Crème Chantilly*

The French are very clever at turning simple things into the spectacular, and this lightly sweetened Whipped Cream is a delicious example. This easy recipe is perfect for filling Cream Puffs (page 142) or serving on top of Cherry Cake (page 148).

Serves 6

ingredients

1 cup heavy cream
⅓ cup confectioners' sugar
1 teaspoon vanilla extract

On your mark, get set, whip!

- Place a 2 1/2- to 3-quart stainless steel bowl and the beaters to an electric hand mixer in the freezer for 10 minutes to chill completely. Make sure the heavy cream is also very cold.

- Pour the cream into the bowl and beat on high speed with the electric hand mixer. Rotate the bowl and move the beaters in a circle as you whip the cream. This will help mix in lots of air as the cream thickens. It will take about 3 to 4 minutes for the cream to thicken properly, so be patient. You will know it's ready when you see ridges from the beaters on the surface of the cream and when soft peaks have formed.

- Turn off the mixer and lift the beaters out of the bowl. If the cream clings to the beaters in soft clouds, it is done; if not, continue beating for another minute.

- After the cream has whipped, add the confectioners' sugar with a flour sifter or hand strainer, gently shaking it over the bowl.

- Add the vanilla and gently fold in the sugar and vanilla with a rubber spatula.

- Keep the whipped cream chilled until ready to serve.

chef's tip

BE CAREFUL WHEN BEATING CREAM NOT TO OVERWHIP IT, OR YOU WILL END UP WITH BUTTER. TURN OFF THE MIXER AND CHECK THE CREAM NOW AND THEN AS YOU WHIP IT. YOU CAN PREPARE THE CREAM UP TO 1 HOUR BEFORE YOU SERVE IT AND IT WILL KEEP ITS SHAPE. REMEMBER TO COVER IT WITH PLASTIC WRAP AND PUT IT IN THE REFRIGERATOR.

Fresh Fruit with Strawberry Glaze
Macedonia con Glassa alle Fragole

Fresh fruits are a very popular part of any Italian meal, so it's no surprise that this famous dessert is loved all over Italy. In choosing fruits for this dish, look for those that are ripe and flavorful, but not too soft. In the summer there is nothing like cold fruit on a hot day. Also, there is nothing like fresh fruit in the fall or winter to remind us of those summer days. Either way, no matter what the season, this is a great dessert.

Serves 6

ingredients

1 cup freshly squeezed orange juice
¼ cup freshly squeezed lemon juice
2 pears
2 apples
2 bananas
4 cups other fresh fruit, such as plums, melon, tangerines, grape fruit, kiwis, peaches, seedless grapes, blueberries, raspberries, or pitted cherries

glaze

½ cup strawberry jam
2 tablespoons freshly squeezed orange juice

On your mark, get set . . .

- Pour 1 cup orange juice into a large bowl. Add the lemon juice.

- Peel the pears and apples, remove the seeds, and cut into chunks. Add them to the bowl.

- Peel and slice the bananas and add to the bowl.

- Wash and prepare the rest of the fruit, removing the skins and seeds where necessary, and measure out 4 cups. Add to the bowl.

Toss!

- Gently toss the fruit, making sure all the pieces are coated with the juices.

- For the glaze, combine the strawberry jam with 2 tablespoons orange juice. Pour over the fruit and toss again until all the fruit is lightly glazed.

- Chill for 1 to 4 hours, but not overnight or the fruit will get soggy. Serve cold.

Cherry Cake *Clafoutis aux Cerises*

This classic cake from Languedoc in the south of France is very popular when cherries are in season. The recipe is easy to make, so it is the perfect finish to any meal. Not cherry season in your neighborhood? You can prepare it with frozen or canned cherries and it will be just as delightful.

Serves 6

ingredients

Filling

½ tablespoon butter

2 tablespoons all-purpose flour

1½ pounds fresh cherries, or 2½ to 3 cups canned or frozen Bing or sweet pitted cherries

Batter

1½ cups whole milk

⅓ cup sugar

3 eggs

2 teaspoons vanilla extract

⅔ cup all-purpose flour

Sauce

1 cup reserved liquid from the fresh or canned cherries

2 tablespoons cherry or raspberry preserves

¼ cup cold water

On your mark ...

• Preheat the oven to 350°F.

• Butter a 5- to 6-cup baking dish or cake pan and dust with 2 tablespoons flour. Tip the dish back and forth to completely cover the entire surface with flour. Invert the dish and tap out any excess flour. Set the dish aside.

• If you are using fresh cherries, wash them and remove the stems. Pit the cherries, using a cherry pitter or small sharp knife. Do this over a bowl to catch any juices that might escape.

• If using canned cherries, drain them and reserve the liquid. Place a couple of layers of paper towels on the counter and carefully pour the drained cherries onto them. Place another sheet of paper towels on top and dry the cherries by rolling them back and forth between the layers.

• If using frozen cherries, there is no need to thaw them; just add 10 minutes to the baking time.

• Measure 2 1/2 to 3 cups cherries and put them in a clean bowl.

Get set . . .

- Add the batter ingredients to the jar of a blender in the order in which they are listed. Place the lid on the jar securely. Blend at high speed for 1 minute.

- To do this by hand, place the ingredients in a large bowl and blend well with a spoon or whisk.

Cook!

- Spread the cherries evenly across the bottom of the baking dish.

- Gently pour the batter over the cherries.

- Bake on the middle rack of the oven for 50 to 60 minutes, or until the top turns golden brown and the center of the cake is firm. Let the cake rest while you prepare the sauce.

- Pour the reserved liquid from the canned cherries or any juices that accumulated from the fresh cherries into a small saucepan.

- Add the cherry or raspberry preserves and the water and mix well.

- Bring to a boil on medium-high heat. Reduce to simmer and cook for 3 to 4 minutes.

- Bring the sauce to the table in a small serving bowl and let your guests spoon it on top of the cake slices.

- This cake is delicious topped with Whipped Cream (page 145) or served just as it is, warm from the oven.

Mexican Celebration Cookies

Polvorones

These cookies are popular all over Mexico and are a favorite dessert at weddings and other celebrations. Their name comes from the Spanish word polvo, which means "dust," and these sweets are so light and delicate that the name is a perfect fit.

Makes 32 cookies

ingredients

2 cups all-purpose flour
1 cup confectioners' sugar
¼ teaspoon salt
1 stick unsalted butter, softened

½ cup vegetable shortening
1 teaspoon pure vanilla extract
1 cup chopped pecans, walnuts, or almonds

On your mark, get set . . .

- Combine the flour, 1/2 cup of the confectioners' sugar, and the salt in a large bowl.

- Sift the dry ingredients into another bowl and set aside.

- Place the softened butter, shortening, and vanilla in a large bowl and beat with an electric hand mixer until smooth.

- Add the dry ingredients and nuts. Combine all the ingredients into a rough dough, using a spoon or very clean hands.

- Remove the dough from the bowl and place on a clean, lightly floured surface. Gently knead into a smooth dough.

- Shape into a ball, wrap in plastic wrap, and chill for at least 1 hour or overnight.

Cook!

- Preheat the oven to 350°F.

- Cut the chilled dough into quarters. Working with one quarter at a time, using your fingertips, shape each quarter into a 7- to 8-inch-long log.

- Cut each log into 8 pieces.

- Form 1 piece into a ball between the palms of your hands and place the balls on an ungreased baking sheet, about 1 inch apart.

- Repeat these steps until all the dough is shaped into cookies.

- Place the baking sheet on the middle rack of the oven and bake for 30 to 35 minutes, or until the cookies are lightly browned.

- When the cookies are baked, let cool slightly. Carefully remove the cookies with a spatula to a rack to cool completely.

- Put the remaining 1/2 cup confectioners' sugar in a wide bowl. Roll the cooled cookies in the sugar to evenly coat them, place them on a plate, and serve.

Chocolate and Walnut Cake

Torta al Cioccolato con Noci

The Italian soil produces many treasures, and walnuts are certainly one of them. Here is a recipe inspired by a classic from the Liguria region of northern Italy. This dessert combines the Italians' love of chocolate and walnuts to create a dense cake that is almost flourless. Serve it with vanilla ice cream or whipped cream and watch it disappear.

Serves 6 to 8

ingredients

2 tablespoons plus 1 teaspoon butter
3 teaspoons plain bread crumbs
1 cup chopped walnuts
8 to 10 ounces milk chocolate with almonds
1⅓ cups confectioners' sugar plus 1 tablespoon for decorating

1 tablespoon all-purpose flour
¼ teaspoon ground cinnamon
4 eggs
1 teaspoon pure vanilla extract
1 tablespoon orange juice
vanilla ice cream or Whipped Cream, page 145, for serving

On your mark . . .

- Preheat the oven to 350°F.

- Grease a 9 x 2-inch round cake pan with 1 teaspoon of the butter.

- Sprinkle the bread crumbs over the bottom of the pan.

- Tip the pan and slowly rotate in a circle, allowing the bread crumbs to evenly cover the entire surface of the pan, sides and bottom. Carefully tap out any excess bread crumbs and discard. Set the pan aside.

- Melt the remaining 2 tablespoons butter in a small saucepan over low heat. Set aside.

Get set . . .

- Pour the chopped walnuts onto a sheet of wax paper.

- Using a rolling pin, crush the walnuts into a coarse powder, but don't overdo it. You still want chunks of walnut left.

On your mark . . .

- Empty the walnuts into a bowl.

- Chop the chocolate into small pieces and add to the walnuts.

- Add 1 1/3 cups of the confectioners' sugar.

- Add the flour and cinnamon and mix well.

- Break the eggs into a separate bowl and add the vanilla and orange juice. Beat the eggs on high speed for about 30 seconds, using an electric hand mixer.

- Add the walnut-chocolate mixture to the eggs and stir with a rubber spatula or wooden spoon until just combined.

- Add the melted butter and give the batter a few more stirs. Do not overmix.

Cook!

- Pour the batter into the cake pan and bake on the middle rack of the oven for 50 to 55 minutes. The cake is done when the middle is firm to the touch and the sides have just begun to pull away from the pan. (After it is baked, the cake will settle to about 1 inch thick.)

- Remove the cake from the oven and place on a rack. Let cool for 10 minutes.

- Run a knife around the edge to loosen it from the sides. Place a dish that is larger than the pan on top. Using hot pads, if you need them, turn the cake pan and the dish upside down. The cake should slip down onto the dish.

- Place the cooling rack on top of the cake and turn the cake over again. Now let it cool completely.

- To decorate, place the remaining 1 tablespoon confectioners' sugar in a hand strainer. Lightly tap the strainer over the cake and let the sugar snow across the top. Or use a shaker and lightly sprinkle the cake with the confectioners' sugar.

- Serve with vanilla ice cream or whipped cream.

essential ingredients in the kitchen

Essential Ingredients in the Kitchen

Allspice
These dried berries are from Jamaica and are available whole or ground. If you have a spice grinder, it is recommended that you buy them whole and grind them yourself for maximum flavor.

Anchovies
This tiny fish packs a large punch of flavor. Anchovies are a very misunderstood ingredient in the Italian kitchen, and unfortunately often get a negative response from people who are afraid to try them. When shopping, look for the anchovies in glass jars, rather than cans. They are larger and have better flavor. Rinse and pat them dry before you use them. If you have any anchovies left over, pack them back in the glass jar and cover with extra virgin olive oil.

Avocados
Avocados are a fruit full of surprises. They are packed with protein and natural oils, and they have been cultivated for over seven thousand years. If they are not ripe when you buy them, they will ripen in a few days if kept out of the sun. You know an avocado is ripe when you gently squeeze it and it is just a little soft, like a tennis ball. When ripe, the fruit's flavor is best described as "buttery." For the recipes in this book, look for the Hass variety. Hass avocados are small and have a dark, slightly bumpy outer skin. To prevent the chopped avocado from turning brown, place the pit in the bowl with the chopped fruit and cover with plastic wrap.

Bacon
Thick-cut smoked bacon is recommended for the recipes in this book.

Balsamic Vinegar
See Vinegar

Bamboo Shoots
Bamboo shoots are just what the name says they are: the young edible shoots of the bamboo tree. They are harvested as soon as they make their first appearance above the ground. Bamboo shoots are available canned. Once you open the can, rinse the shoots under cold running water to remove any bitter flavor. They are already cooked, so they are perfect for fast-cooking stir-fried dishes. Once opened, they will keep for about two weeks in a closed container of fresh water. The water should be changed two or three times a week to ensure freshness.

Basil
Look for fresh basil that is bright green and has no dark spots. Use only the leaves of this herb, not the stems. There are many varieties of basil to choose from, even red. Red basil is called opal, and it will work as well as green with all the recipes in this book. Basil leaves can hold dirt. Wash them well, then pat them dry. The best way to use basil is not to cut it with a knife. Tear it with your fingers and you will not bruise it.

Bean Sprouts

Bean sprouts have been a part of Chinese cuisine for more than three thousand years. They are very nutritious and fun to eat. There are two varieties of bean sprouts. The mung bean sprout is white in color, chubby, and very crunchy. The soybean sprout is longer, and it has a tiny soybean at the end. Buy sprouts fresh and keep them in a clean plastic bag. It is a good idea to punch some holes in the bag, so the sprouts will have air. Buy only the amount you need, because sprouts don't keep much longer than three or four days.

Bread Crumbs

The best bread crumbs are the ones you make yourself. Old bread that has hardened makes really good crumbs. Grate it with a hand grater, using the tiniest holes. Be careful not to grate your knuckles along with the bread. You can also buy bread crumbs. Look for the ones marked "plain." They will have no salt or extra seasoning. That way you can season them yourself.

Butter

French butter is made from cream and is usually unsalted. American butter comes unsalted (sweet) or salted. If you are more familiar with salted butter, use it for the recipes in this book.

Capers

These are buds or blooms from a Mediterranean shrub that have been preserved and packed in vinegar or salt water. The ones packed in salt water generally taste better. No matter which ones you get, you must rinse them several times before you use them. Look for the larger-size capers rather than the small ones; they will have more flavor.

Chiles

Read all about fresh and dried chiles on page 92.

Chives

A member of the onion family, chives taste best when fresh and not dried. Their flavor is more delicate than onions. Chives also make a colorful garnish.

Cilantro

Cilantro is an herb also known as fresh coriander or Chinese parsley. It adds great flavor to Mexican dishes. Cilantro looks almost identical to parsley and is easily confused with it, but it has a bolder flavor and a spicy aroma. It should be washed to remove any sand still clinging to the stems or leaves. Wrapped in plastic, it will keep for about a week in the refrigerator.

Cooking Oils

Peanut and sesame oils are very common in Chinese cooking, and they add a lot of flavor to many dishes. Peanut oil is used for stir-frying and deep-frying because it has a high smoking point, which means that it can cook at high temperatures before it begins to smoke. Sesame oil, which is made from sesame seeds that have been toasted and pressed, is more delicate and is added to dishes for its rich flavor. It smokes very quickly, however, and is not recommended for high temperatures. The Chinese cook often pours a small amount of sesame oil on steamed fish before serving to add delicious flavor. Another good oil to use for frying is canola. Canola oil is lighter in flavor than peanut oil and a little lower in saturated fat and calories.

Cream, Heavy
There are different grades of cream ranging from light to heavy, depending on the fat content. Heavy cream is at least 35 percent fat. When buying cream, look for the "sell by" date furthest from the day you purchase it. If possible, avoid buying ultra-pasteurized cream, which can be hard to whip. To successfully whip cream, it is very important to chill the beaters, bowl, and the cream thoroughly before starting.

Dijon Mustard
The city of Dijon in central France is famous for its mustard. Made from three different seeds from the cabbage family, Dijon mustard is pale yellow and full flavored. After you open a jar of mustard, keep it in the refrigerator and it will last several months.

Dried Beans
Beans are one of the most common ingredients in Mexican cooking. Dried red pinto beans are very common in northern Mexico and black beans are more common in the south. Both varieties will work for the recipes in this book. Rinse beans in a colander and then pour them onto a tray in a single layer. Carefully check for and remove any tiny stones or shriveled, very dark beans.

Egg Roll Wrappers
Egg roll wrappers can be bought in the supermarket. Once you open the package, use the amount you need and freeze the rest. As you work with the wrappers, make sure to keep them covered, or they will dry out. If they are frozen, thaw them fully before using. You can substitute spring roll wrappers for egg roll wrappers. Spring roll wrappers are not made with eggs, so they are thinner and a little harder to work with.

Garlic
Garlic is a member of the onion family and is a valuable flavor maker in French cooking. When you purchase garlic, look for large bulbs that are hard and solid. Inside the bulb are cloves. To use the cloves, first separate them from the bulb. With the flat side of a knife, give them a good whack, then remove the white paperlike skin and cut off the dark tip. The cloves can be chopped into small pieces, mashed, or cut into thin slices. A garlic press is a great way to extract flavor from the cloves. Many nutritionists believe that garlic has great health benefits because it is rich in minerals. The world is divided into two groups of people: those who love garlic and those who don't. Which are you?

Ginger or Ginger Root
Ginger is a very important spice in Chinese cooking. When you shop for fresh ginger, look for a nice smooth skin and no dark spots. Peel off the outer skin with a potato peeler. Then slice off the amount the recipe calls for, using a sharp

knife. Tightly wrap the remaining piece in plastic wrap and refrigerate. Ginger will keep in the refrigerator for up to two weeks. It can also be frozen. You can use a garlic press to crush ginger. A grater also works to get the juice out of it. Ginger is spicy and too much can make a dish hot, so be careful when you use it.

Hoisin Sauce

This thick, sweet sauce is made from soybeans, spices, mild chilies, and sugar. Be careful not to confuse it with plum sauce or fish sauce, which have quite different flavors. Once you open the jar, refrigerate it. It will keep for up to six months.

Lard

Lard is pork fat that is cooked down into a solid by a process called rendering. Many people are reluctant to use lard because they believe that it is very high in cholesterol and fat. Actually, according to the USDA, lard has only half the cholesterol and two-thirds the saturated fat of butter. Today the modern Mexican cook uses lard in moderation, and you should, too. Consider buying lard only if you are able to find it fresh from a Mexican grocer, because commercially produced lard is made with hydrogenated oils and is not recommended. Vegetable, canola, and corn oil are excellent substitutes.

Masa Harina

Masa harina is a specially ground cornmeal and is the basic ingredient in tortillas. It is generally available in the baking section of your local supermarket. Quick-cooking grits are an excellent substitute. Once the package is opened, place the masa harina in an airtight container and it will keep for up to a year.

Mexican Chocolate

The chocolate of Mexico comes in different sizes and shapes. Harder and coarser than other chocolates, it is sweetened and flavored with cinnamon and sometimes ground nuts. The most common packaging is a box of six 3-ounce tablets or disks, which are perforated into pie-shaped wedges. Mexican chocolate is available in supermarkets or specialty food stores.

Mozzarella Cheese

A delicate white cheese made from cow's or buffalo's milk. It melts wonderfully and is an important ingredient in many Italian dishes. It is available in Italian specialty markets or cheese stores. You can also purchase mozzarella at almost any supermarket. If you buy it fresh, use it the same day or no later than the next day. If you buy it packaged, be sure to check the expiration date.

Niçoise Olives

Niçoise olives are small and black with pits and come from Nice, in the south of France. They are cured in saltwater, or brine, for up to six months. Niçoise olives can usually be found in specialty food stores. Black olives, either Greek or Italian, are a good substitute.

Nutmeg

This spice is native to Indonesia. If used in moderation, it gives dishes a warm, soft flavor. But be careful! Nutmeg can be an overpowering flavor, so don't over-do it. It is best to buy it whole and grate only what you need for your recipe. Store it sealed in a glass jar and it will keep a long time.

Olive Oil, Extra-Virgin

Olive oil is called "extra virgin" if it has been obtained from the first pressing of the olives without the use of chemicals and has low acidity (less than 1 percent). It also has great flavor. Cold-pressed extra-virgin olive oil is regarded as the best of the extra-virgin oils. If the oil is "cold-pressed," that means the olives were pressed without heat, so the oil keeps its flavor. In salad dressings, the flavor of good olive oil will enhance any salad you make. It is important to note that extra-virgin oil can be expensive and so you must consider your budget when buying it. Keep olive oil away from bright sunlight and stored in cool temperatures.

Oregano

Dried or fresh, this pungent herb is full of flavor. It is perfect for pizza, tomato sauces, chicken dishes, and vegetables. Be careful not to overdo it. Too much oregano can overpower a dish. Used sparingly, it is an essential part of the flavor of Italian cooking. Dried oregano, stored in a covered glass jar, will keep for about six months.

Oyster Sauce

Made from oysters and spices, oyster sauce has had a place in the Chinese kitchen for hundreds of years. Once you open the bottle, keep it refrigerated and it will stay fresh for up to six months.

Paprika

Paprika is a spice made from dried sweet red peppers. It is usually added to a recipe not only for its flavor but also for its appealing red color.

Parmigiano-Reggiano

This golden cheese is so famous in Italy that it has its own set of laws to regulate how it should be made. Once you taste it, you will know why it is called the "king of Italian cheese." Parmigiano-Reggiano has been made for over five hundred years, but the official recipe used today in Parma and Reggio Emilia was only established in 1955. It is lower in fat and cholesterol than many other cheeses. You can recognize it easily because its name is always stamped into the rind of the cheese. It is best to buy it in a wedge and grate it as you need it to keep it at peak flavor. To store, wrap in wax paper and then aluminum foil and keep in the coldest part of the refrigerator. Parmigiano-Reggiano is expensive, so consider your budget when shopping for it. You may substitute Parmesan cheese, but try not to buy it already grated.

Parsley, Flat-Leaf

This variety of parsley is preferable for cooking because it has more flavor than curly-leaf parsley. Look for bright green leaves and stems that are not wilted or shriveled. Be sure you don't make a common mistake and buy fresh cilantro, a similar-looking herb. Wash the parsley before you use it, and chop it, using only the leaves to get the best flavor.

Pepper, Whole Black

There is a real difference in the flavor of black pepper when it is freshly ground. You are probably most familiar with the ground pepper that you buy in the store. Chances are it was ground months earlier and the flavor has diminished. Grinding your own peppercorns requires a pepper mill. Use pepper with caution because it can overpower the flavor of a dish and make it very hot.

Plums, Dried
Prunes are dried plums. The natural sweetness makes them a flavorful addition to French recipes. When shopping for dried plums, look for those that are minimally processed, pitted, and don't have large amounts of chemical additives.

Queso Fresco
Queso fresco means "fresh cheese." It is an important element in Mexican cooking because of its subtle flavor. Queso fresco is available in Mexican markets or specialty cheese stores. Keep it refrigerated and well wrapped. It should be used within three to five days of purchase.

Radicchio
This plant is a member of the chicory family. A head of radicchio is small—just a little larger than an orange—and has delicate red and white lettucelike leaves. Radicchio makes a great addition to any salad. Look for firm, solid heads with no wilted or brown leaves. Wash the leaves and pat them dry with paper towels or dry in a salad spinner. Belgian endive is a good substitute.

Sesame Seeds
These tiny, nutty, very flavorful seeds have been used in Chinese cooking for centuries. Sesame seeds may be black, white, yellow, or brown, and they are often toasted for added flavor.

Shallots
These delicate, small bulbs come from the onion family. Their flavor is much softer than garlic, but their appearance is similar. The flavor of a shallot is released when it is cooked. Shallots should be stored in a cool, dry place out of the sun. They will remain fresh for about three to four weeks after you purchase them.

Shiitake Mushrooms
These mushrooms come fresh or dried. You must soak the dried mushrooms in warm or hot water for at least thirty minutes to revive them. Dried shiitake mushrooms give your recipes a deep, smoky flavor. They will keep for a very long time in an airtight container. A glass jar with a lid works well for storing dried mushrooms.

Soy Sauce
For three thousand years, soy sauce has flavored the foods of China. There are two main types of soy sauce, light and dark. Both are rich and delicious. Soy sauce has many uses, but be careful—too much can overpower the flavor of a dish. An opened bottle of sauce will keep at room temperature for six to nine months.

Tomatillos
Tomatillos are a small, green, tart-tasting fruit. They are often confused with green tomatoes. The papery outer husk needs to be peeled away and removed before using, and then the fruit should be washed to remove any sticky residue. Look for firm, solid tomatillos that fill the skin completely. They will keep in the refrigerator for several weeks.

Tomatoes

There is no doubt that tomatoes are the key ingredient in a lot of Italian cooking. When shopping for fresh tomatoes, look for a nice rich, red color and avoid the fruits with spots or bruises. If you are unable to find good fresh tomatoes, don't hesitate to buy canned. To store fresh tomatoes, keep them away from heat, but never put them in the refrigerator. The cold will destroy their flavor and texture.

Tortillas

Mexican tortillas usually contain just corn flour (called masa) and water. Tortillas made with wheat flour are also popular, especially in northern Mexico. Tortillas may be available in supermarkets or specialty food stores. Look for ones that are made without chemical preservatives or added fats. If you have a Mexican specialty store near you, chances are you will find excellent tortillas. Keep them well wrapped and refrigerated for up to a week after purchase. They also freeze very well. Thaw frozen tortillas before attempting to separate them.

Vinegar

Balsamic vinegar is from the Emilia-Romagna region in northern Italy. Balsamic has been made in this region for over a thousand years. There are many grades of balsamic vinegar and prices can range from inexpensive to very costly. The price and quality are determined by the age of the vinegar and where it originated. Inexpensive balsamic will work quite well for the recipes in this book.

Red wine vinegar is very popular in salad dressings in Italy. It has a deep, rich flavor. Look for red wine vinegar that is bright red and not cloudy.

cooking terms

Cooking Terms

Here are a few simple cooking techniques to keep in mind as you prepare the recipes in this book:

Blanch
To plunge vegetables into a pot of boiling water for a minute or two to lightly cook them and help keep their color from fading.

Chop
To chop means to use a sharp knife to cut food into pieces. Chopping vegetables for recipes can seem like a lot of work. A food processor, if there is one in your kitchen, can make food preparation tasks easier. Ask an adult assistant to help you use the food processor, and be very careful of the sharp blades.

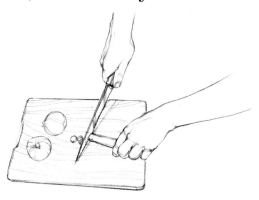

Fold
To gently blend lighter ingredients with heavier ones so that they are not overmixed.

Pan-fry
This is a way to fry food in small amounts of oil. Pan-frying will brown and crisp food.

Reduce
To boil a liquid at a high temperature until it has partly evaporated. Reducing is used to thicken sauces without having to add any extra fat or flour.

Sauté
To lightly fry ingredients in a small amount of fat, butter, or oil, while stirring with a spoon or spatula.

Simmer

To cook food in a liquid at just below the boiling point. Gentle bubbles roll lazily to the top of the liquid that is simmering. The technique of simmering brings out maximum flavor and is used frequently in French cooking.

Skim

To remove fats or cooking residues as ingredients go from raw to cooked. In making soups or sauces, skimming is an important step in reducing fat and enriching flavor.

Stir-fry

The Chinese invented the technique of stir-frying for a very good reason: to save fuel. Chinese chefs did not have unlimited amounts of cooking fuel thousands of years ago, so they created some basic rules for cooking that still work perfectly today. Stir-frying is a simple cooking technique. But a successful stir-fry is not something that just happens. It takes planning and preparation. If you stick to the rules, the rewards are huge!

- Cut the main ingredients into fairly small pieces as described in the recipe. Cut them so that they are all about the same size. That way everything will cook more evenly and be done at the same time.

- After you have cut, sliced, minced, or chopped the ingredients, line them up near the wok in the order that you will use them. When you start to stir-fry, there is no time to run around the kitchen looking for tools and ingredients. Have everything that you need ready, so when you start to cook, you won't have to look!

- Preheat your wok* for about thirty seconds on high or medium-high heat (to be sure that the food cooks evenly). Then add the oil. Many recipes follow with garlic or ginger, for flavoring.

166

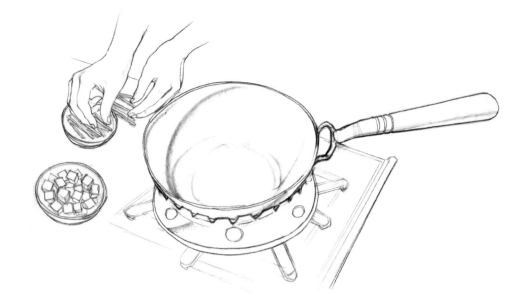

- The main ingredients, such as the meat or fish, usually go in next. They will make a sizzling noise as they come in contact with the hot cooking surface. Use a long-handled metal spoon or Chinese spatula to move the ingredients around. After the main ingredients are almost completely cooked, remove them and reheat the wok. Next, stir-fry the vegetables. The vegetables that need more time to cook are added first and those that need less time are added last. Green beans or carrots, for example, take longer to cook than green onions or spinach.

- Now add the seasonings and the cooking liquids such as chicken, beef, or vegetable stock.

- Some recipes call for adding cornstarch, dissolved in a liquid, at the end. It thickens and finishes the dish.

    *Note: If you don't have a wok, you can use a ten- or twelve-inch frying pan with a cover instead. It will work just as well for all the recipes in this book.

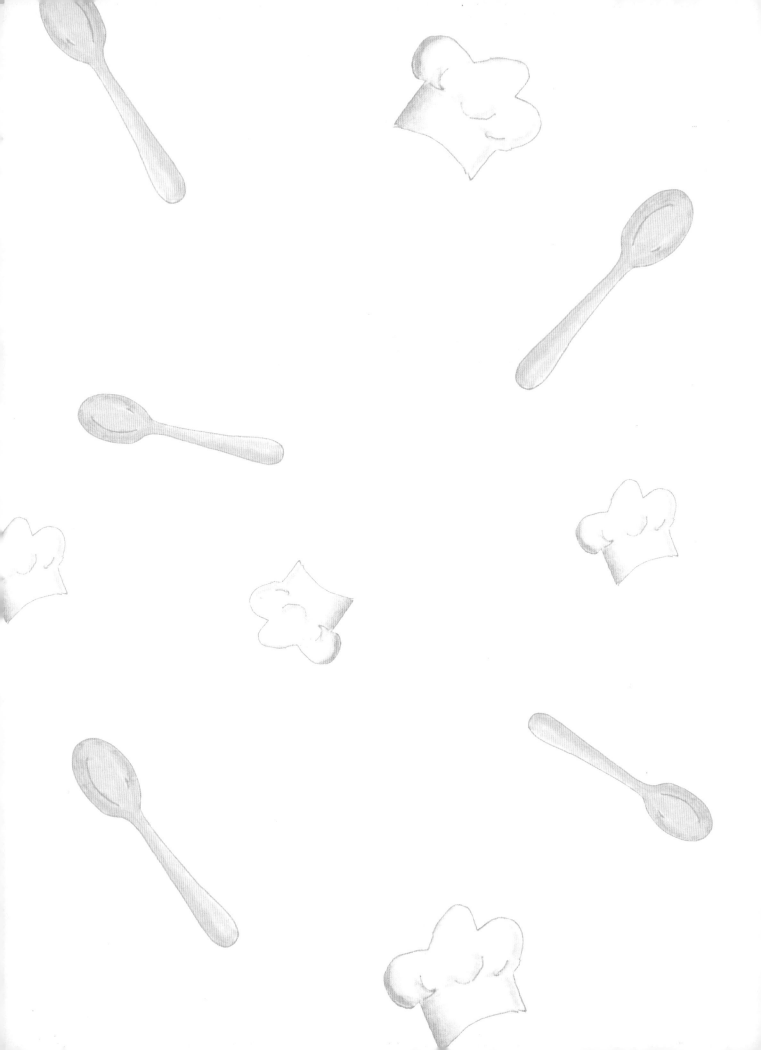

cooking equipment and utensils

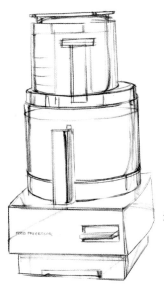

food processor

pizza pan

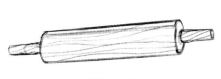

rolling pin

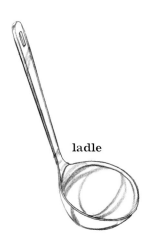

ladle

chinese spatula

This is a very handy cooking tool. It looks like the spatulas used in Western kitchens but has a longer handle and a slightly rounded front edge. The edge is shaped to match the wok's rounded form, so it is just right for stir-frying.

chinese dipper

The dipper looks just like a soup ladle, except it is a little wider. It is used to ladle out liquids or to add them while you cook.

chinese strainer

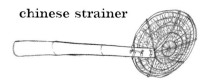

A strainer is used to lift foods out of liquids. The Chinese strainer has a bamboo handle that will not get hot when you use it.

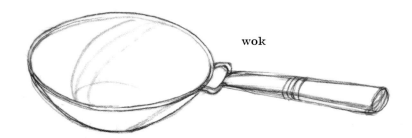

wok

The wok is one of the oldest cooking utensils in the world. It dates back thousands of years. The wok is also the most versatile cooker you can use, because it allows you to stir-fry, deep-fry, steam, and even smoke ingredients. Most importantly, it concentrates the heat in just the right way so that foods cook quickly. Most woks today are made out of rolled carbon steel, light iron, or stainless steel. There are also electric woks with nonstick surfaces, but they are not as popular, and they can never get as hot as the traditional wok.

The Chinese wok is shaped like a large bowl, with high sides, either a flat or a round bottom, and a long wooden handle.

If you have an electric stove, you should use a flat-bottom wok, because it will stand on the burner better. By adding a wok ring, you can use a round-bottom wok on an electric stove. The best way to use a wok on an electric stove is to keep one burner—preferably the one next to the burner you are using—free of pots. That way, if the heat gets too high, you can move the wok to the empty, cold burner.

When shopping for a wok, look for one that is fourteen inches in diameter. Follow the manufacturer's instructions for seasoning the cooking surface, and your wok will last for years of perfect meals.

The cover for a wok is generally made out of aluminum and has a handle on top. Covering the wok makes it the perfect utensil for steaming or boiling.

wok cover

The wok ring keeps the wok from moving or sliding while you cook. If you have a round-bottom wok, don't use it without the ring.

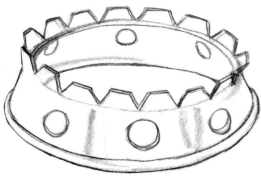

wok ring

mixing bowl

tongs

baking sheet

cheese grater

rubber or latex kitchen gloves

metal colander

strainer

wire cooling rack

saucepans with lids

round potato masher

salad spinner

potato peeler

cutting board

baking pan

large metal
slotted spoon

spatula

vegetable brush

blender

electric hand mixer

stockpot with lid

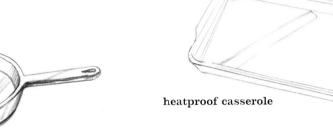
heatproof casserole

cherry pitter

cast-iron skillet (frying pan)

whisk

meat thermometer

roasting pan

Deep-fry thermometer

assorted knives

skillets (frying pans)

flour sifter

Index